Syriza:Neo-Liberals in Disguise

DEDICATION

The book is dedicated to the hundreds of thousands who occupied the squares for two months on their own without the active political participation of the bankrupt political leaderships of all the present political parties of Greece.

CONTENTS

TIMELINE OF GREEK CRISIS

2009

- **4 October 2009** – The centre-left PASOK wins the Greek legislative elections. The party received 43.92% of the popular vote and 160 of 300 parliamentary seats. The main 'electoral programme was there is money'

- **20 October 2009** – George Papaconstantinou, finance minister in Greece's new socialist government, disclosed that the nation's deficit would soar this year to almost 12.5 per cent of gross domestic product.

- **22 October 2009** – Fitch rating agency downgrades Greece's credit rating to A- from A.
- **8 December 2009** – Fitch rating agency downgrades Greece's credit rating to BBB+ from A-.

- **16 December 2009** – Standard and Poor's rating agency downgrade Greece's credit rating.

- **23 December 2009** – Moody's rating agency downgrades Greece to A2 category from A1.

2010

- **9 February 2010** – The parliament approved the first austerity package measures that included a freeze in the salaries of all government employees, a 10% cut in bonuses, as well as cuts in overtime workers.

- **3 March 2010** – The parliament passed a new major austerity package measures. The measures included: Pensions freezes, an increase in sales tax from 19% to 21%, rises in taxes on fuel, cigarettes and alcohol, rises in taxes on luxury goods, cuts in public sector pay.

- **9 April 2010** – Fitch downgraded Greek credit rating to BBB-minus category from BBB+.[
- **22 April 2010** – Moody's downgraded Greece's credit rating to A3 from A2.

- **23 April 2010** – George Papandreou, Greece's prime minister formally requested an international bailout. The financing will come from an emergency aid package with the participation of European Union, European Central Bank andInternational Monetary Fund.

- **27 April 2010** – Standard and Poor's downgraded Greece's credit ratings below investment grade to junk bond status.

- **28 April 2010** – Greek/German 10-year debt yield spread surpassed 1000 basis points.

- **2 May 2010** – Papandreou, the IMF, and euro-zone leaders agree to a €110 billion ($143 billion) bailout package that would take effect over the next three years. The government announced the new austerity package measures.

- **5 May 2010** – General nationwide strike and demonstrations in two major cities in Greece turned violent. Four people were killed when **allegedly a group** of masked people threw petrol bombs in a Marfin Egnatia Bank branch on Stadiou street. This was a govt provocation to weaken movement.

- **6 May 2010** – The Greek parliament passed the

new austerity package measures. The bill passed with 172 votes in favour and 121 against, with the votes of governing party (without three deputies) and the party LAOS.

- **14 June 2010** – Moody's downgraded Greece's credit rating to Ba1 from A3.

- **7 July 2010** – Parliament passes pension reform, a key requirement of the EU/IMF.

- **15 December 2010** – The parliament passed the law for public companies. The law sets a cap on wage monthly as well as cuts by 10 percent the salaries above 1,800 euro.

- **23 December 2010** – Greece's parliament approved the 2011 austerity budget.

2011

- **14 January 2011** – Fitch downgraded Greek credit rating to BB+ from BBB-.

- **7 March 2011** – Moody's downgraded Greek credit rating to B1 from Ba1.

- **29 March 2011** – Standard and Poor's downgraded Greek credit rating to BB minus.

- **9 May 2011** – Standard and Poor's downgraded Greek credit rating to B from BB minus.
- **20 May 2011** – Fitch downgraded Greek credit rating to B+ from BB+.

- **25 May 2011** – The Greek Indignant Citizens

Movement also known as Square Movement was started the daily protests. It was inspired by Spanish similar movement.

- **1 June 2011** – Moody's downgrades Greece to Caa1 from B1.

- **13 June 2011** – Standard and Poor's downgraded Greece in lowest rated.[

- **15th June 2011-** Greek General Strike, wide use of tear gas, Papandreou announces a resignation in the lull of protests but New Democracys Samaras refuses to take the reigns

- **17 June 2011** – The prime minister made a broad cabinet reshuffle. Evangelos Venizelos assumed new Finance Minister.

- **29 June 2011** – The Greek parliament passed the new austerity package measures despite the big protests outside the parliament building. The two-day demonstrations against the bill, turned violent as protestors clashed with police in front of the Greek parliament and other areas of central Athens. The bill passed with 155 votes in favour and 138 against. The measures included new taxes and new cuts of worker's wages.

- **July 2011** – Fitch downgraded Greek credit rating to CCC from B+.

- **25 July 2011** – Moodys downgraded Greek credit rating to Ca- category.

- **27 July 2011** – Standard and Poor's downgraded

Greece to CC level from CCC.

- **8 August 2011** – The bourse's general index fell below the 1000 points, the lowest level since January 1997.

- **11 September 2011** – The government imposed a new property tax that be collected through electricity bill.

- **20 October 2011** – Greece government passed the multi-austerity bill, amid protests and violent riots outside the parliament building.

- **27 October 2011** – The investors agreed a "haircut" of 50% in converting their existing bonds into new loans.

- **28 October 2011** – An anti-austerity protest in Thessaloniki forced the cancellation of the Military parade on the commemoration of 28th October (OXI – No day known as Greeces defeat of Mussolinis Italy). Similar facts occurred in several other Greek cities.

- **31 October 2011** – Greek Prime Minister George Papandreou called for a confidence vote and a referendum to approve last week's EU summit deal about the Greek debt haircut.

- **4 November 2011** – George Papandreou won the confidence vote with 153 votes in favour and 145 votes against.

- **6 November 2011** – Prime Minister George Papandreou resigned.

- **10 November 2011** – Lucas Papademos ex-Goldman Sachs Banker became the New Greek Prime Minister, leader of the three party's coalition government, consisted by parties PASOK, ND and LAOS.

- **December 2011** – Greece's private TV channel Alter stopped broadcasting due to financial difficulties.

2012

- **12 February 2012** – The parliament passed a new austerity package measures amid violent protests. Many buildings in the centre of Athens were burnt during the riots.[52][53]

- **9 March 2012** – The private sector participation reached 83,5% of Greek bond holders.

- **4 April 2012** – A retired pharmacist commits suicide a short distance from Greece's parliament as an act of protest against austerity politics. He immediately becomes a symbol for groups opposing the austerity measures, and violent clashes between police and demonstrators erupt in Athens.[54]

- **6 May 2012** – The election was held. The New Democracy party won but it reduced its rates. The governing party PASOK collapsed while radical left party and far right party had increase of their rates.

Neither of the parties won the majority of the parliament seats. So was announced early election in June.[55]

- **16 May 2012** – Panagiotis Pikramenos assumed a caretaker Prime Minister.[56]

- **25 May 2012** – The bourse general index fell below the 500 points.[57]

- **17 June 2012** – The early election was held. The New Democracy party won with a 29.7% of votes but didn't concentrate the majority of the parliament seats. Four days later, it formed a coalition government with the participation New Democracy, PASOK and DIMAR (breakaway from Syriza). Antonis Samaras, the president of New Democracy, became the new Prime Minister of Greece. Syriza came second with 27.8%

- **5 November 2012** – The Greek parliament adopted a new round of austerity cuts that are required for Greece to receive the next instalment of the international economic bailout. A big protest occurred outside the parliament.[60][61]

- **11 November 2012** – Greece passes the 2013 austerity budget.[62]

2013

- **28 April 2013** – The parliament approved a bill that included cut some 15,000 state jobs by the end of next year, including 4,000 in 2013.

- **11 June 2013** – The Greek government closed

down the country's Public Broadcasting Service ERT.

- **21 June 2013** – Democratic Left withdrew from Greek coalition government. The government kept a razor-thin majority in parliament.

-

- **24 June 2013** – Greek Prime Minister Antonis Samaras reshuffled his cabinet.[67]

- **17 July 2013** – The Greek parliament approves new austerity measures including a contentious plan for thousands of layoffs and wage cuts for civil service workers.

- **21 December 2013** –The bill about the new tax property and the auction of houses was approved by a majority of 152 deputies in the 300-seat chamber.

- **To date there have been 37 General Strikes only two have been 48hour strikes. No single measure has to date been repealed in relation to wage cuts, pension cuts and mass sackings**

The Rise of Syriza in Greece: Neo-Liberals in Disguise

The EU's Last Chance?

The roots of Syriza originate from a split in the KKE in 1968 during the American military junta that ruled Greece from 1967-74.

Their political traditions centred on a 'liberal' communism influenced by events in E Europe (Prague Spring etc) and the struggles for democracy in Greece in the mid-60's when they had formed a legal front called EDA which gained 25% of the votes in the late 1950's.

When the KKE was legalised many ex-KKE members who had been forced into exile in the SU due to the British-American backed civil war in the late 1940's, came back and joined the more liberal wing of the communists.

1989-Governing with the New Democracy then PASOK

Despite the differences and apart from them in 1989 they joined an electoral front with the KKE known as Sinaspismos and subsequently joined the government of the Right, New Democracy, allegedly to bury the hatchet of the cold war and to put an end to the corruption of PASOK and Andreas Papandreou but in reality to make known to the world that the fake Greek Left had become …American.

Main characters from the Left in this government were Kouvelis-now leader of the Dem Left who became a Minister, Dragasakis (main operator of Syriza) and Lafazanis who was a close collaborator of Florakis (leader of the then KKE) as he was famous for being in the student occupation of the Athens Law school which triggered the fall of the junta.

From the mid-90s to the mid-2000 the fortunes of Sinaspismos were pretty dire and they opened up the electoral subsidy to other groups on the far left and many joined them to get a slice of the pie. In 2004 Sinaspismos wouldn't have received more than 3% so it was pretty obvious as they would lose their state subsidy. Alavanos who had taken over from the corporate lawyer a few years before (Konstantopoulos) was astute enough to bring in a young lad from the organisation to do the negotiating, but was soon pushed out of his leading role by the same young man called Alexis Tsipras.

Their political line can be characterised as 'left' globalists. They are very strong on the issues of the self: rights of individuals above the collective. The 'rights' of immigrants above Greeks, of 'women' above men, of the EU above all despite having some shady characters in their midst. The corporate controlled media keep a lid on many scandals by politicians and only reveal them when they need to (ie if they step out of line or the balance of class forces changes unfavourably in any way for the ruling class). The Greek corporate controlled media is part and parcel of the big state capitalist interests that run Greece. Bobolas who owns the Ethnos daily is big on 'scandals' but never his own (Keratea land fill, road tolls, Gold Mine Skouries). The Greek media are the rabid dogs of capitalism in decay. Anyone who says anything and sticks their head above the parapet is shot down and labelled.

The label *'radical left'* to Syriza has been assigned by themselves and the corporate media around the world. They are as *'radical'* and *'left'* as Tony Bliar was. He stood on platforms on CND in the early 80's but had no ideological problem leading the invasion of Iraq side by side with the Texan oil-igarchs around Bush. Syriza has governed previously with the hard right of Greece (Mitsotakis) in the late 80's where the memories of the junta and the civil war were still fresh in people's minds. They don't have **any ideological hangups.** Principles years ago were left at the door. They can be characterised simply as a collection of sailors who will adapt the sails and take themselves wherever the wind blows. In their eyes it is to make the biggest accommodation to the capitalist system possible.

PASOK-ND Disintegrating

A whole host of ex-members of PASOK and trade unionist officials have decamped the sinking ship that ruled for four decades in post-Junta Greece and joined Syriza. Famous names are Dourou (who was in the close circle of ex-Defence Minister Tzohatsopoulos of PASOK), Sakorafa (ex-Olympian Champion) and Kouroumblis (blind MP) Glezos (PASOK). Attempting to create a new PASOK under today's conditions will be an impossible task only because the mantra of our times is globalisation (constantly expanding the EU until it reaches Asia) and importing a constant array of goods (latest being non-patented medicines to shut down the Greek pharmaceutical industry). A political vacuum has been created and it has to be filled. Careerists of all sorts are jumping on the most popular bandwagon to try to survive and cover up past sins. PASOK and ND bankrupted Greece, any serious left wing party that opened its doors to this rot from the past does not want to correct things but try to continue them in a different social set up.

Strikewave

Despite being labelled as far left Syriza as a leader of the opposition has done everything in its power to derail and collapse strikes not seeking to ride on a wave of popular anger should it come to power pre-maturely and then have to implement what it has promised (restoration of previous minimum wage, jobs back from mass sackings etc.) though to be fair to them they have watered down immensely what they can offer not really offering to give jobs back to the 1.5million officially unemployed or to pay any form of assistance to them. They are playing the long parliamentary game refusing to leave Parliament despite stating that the govt runs on Executive Decrees (22 so far) and by passing normal Parliamentary procedure. During the Metro Workers strike they didn't criticise the sellout leadership of Stamatopoulos who stood on the Antarsya electoral ticket and during the mass teachers strikes their leadership caved in.

In the ERT occupation they campaigned against the view of getting their own MP's to occupy it and call other workers out as 'extremism' and the candidate they supported in the journalists union who was for OpenERT (state broadcaster) months later changed position and supported the creation of the scab TV- NERIT accepting that not all the 3,000 employees would be re-hired. (i)

Alongside the KKE they have a majority in the Public Sectors Union-ADEDY and during December 2013 they held a rally whereby only 100 union officials turned up. This signifies what they have been doing all along. Appearing militant in speeches and when the balance of forces change and they are thrusted into positions of authority they do nothing or exactly the same as the previous leaderships before.

Lafazanis ex-KKE Syrizas fake left within the fake Left

The role of the fake left within Syriza is held by Lafazanis who holds 30% of the votes at the Syriza conference (2013) and recently came out in support of a return to the Drachma.(ii) He appeared with the KKE right at the beginning of ND assumption of power when the KKE sold out the steelworkers strikes at the mass rally announcing a return to work. In a public meeting before this time with a university lecturer from abroad he publically stated how would the Left cope when informing the workers that they have to take even more wage cuts. In other words where their ex-members went (DemLeft) ie in a coalition with ND-PASOK between June 2012 till June 2013 Lafazanis was already contemplating. Unless one is able to confront the global banksters head on ie annul all debt payments until an international audit is held and go over to a militarised economy once the banksters freeze the country from the international banking system there will be no let up in the crisis continuing unabated until those that work are on Bangladeshi wage rates and those unemployed scavenge in dustbins whilst pensions (become Chinese ie non-existent) and all medical care (becomes American) is phased out from the state sector. Tsipras moral authority originates from Lafazanis in other words Tsipras could not appear as being part of the 'radical left' without Lafazanis and vice versa. They supplement and complement each other in all their political machinations. Tsipras goes abroad and lectures in all the circuits of global imperialism whilst Lafazanis gives militant speeches back home. It's a circus act, a double act for mass consumption. But guess what, people ain't buying as evidenced by the No Confidence Vote by Syriza in December. A mass rally was held in Sindagma Square and only one section was barely filled by the party that got 27% (18 months previously).

In order to justify the 'left' face of Lafazanis and lets remember the heady days of 1989-1990 when the KKE governed with ND in order to clean the augean stables of PASOK fraud and today we have the same allegedly similar demand (prosecute politicians for bribery scandals eg Siemens, Vatopedi etc) he remained in Sinaspismos (precusrsor to Syriza) whilst the youth wing of the KKE left, condemning the coalition governments as being sellouts. Lafazani has no problem governing with New Democracy or its offshoot (Independent Greeks) or accepting hundreds of ex-PASOK functionaries. To push the left face he invited over Costas Lapavitsas as explained by Stathis Kouvelakis in New Left Review Nov-Dec 2011 to promote debt default, exit from the EZ (but in reality that is just to keep on board the myriad of sects that joined Syriza and they need them to campaign for the majority's pro-EU policies).

As an aside when in early 2011 both Stathis Kouvelakis and Costas Lapavitsas were asked about a return to a national currency in a meeting in London they both stated this was ridiculous, out of the question and we may be referred to as being the 'taliban in support of the drachma'. So their positions are essentially based on media perceptions, not principles. Three years later in public opinion polls show 1 in 4 of Greek citizens are for the return of a national currency and two organisations have been created to service those interests (Plan B, Drachma Party) and Lafazanis inside Syriza has stated he is in support now of an exit from the EZ and a return to the Drachma.

The next fallback option for capitalism is being created now, for after all both Alavanos (Plan B) and Katsanaevas (Drachma Party) are stalwarts of Maastricht and the EU, Katsanevas was the Social Security Chief in the 80's under Papandreou.

A return to the Drachma cannot in and of itself solve the crisis. It is only a first step in a new direction with other measures necessary to bring back jobs. This cannot happen in a globalised market where imports are in a free for all. The critique of 'nationalism' in todays globalised world is created by the political forces allied with the large transnationals that rule the world. No national economy can rebuild itself if it isn't working and no company can compete if they can't sell as they are being constantly undercut by raw material and labour costs (sometimes $1/100^{th}$ of existing ones) In other words an annulment of the debts a return to a national currency and an Exit Left from the EU are part of re-orientating Greece away from the Western sphere of influence and doing business with countries that do business, not just live like parasites off Greek peoples blood. But this isn't why Syriza rose to prominence by default. They are there to continue *in a new form* the same old politics, notwithstanding the corporate media portrayal as 'radical leftists' and their 'far left' hangers on the world over.

On the EU

It's no coincidence that this year represents the centenary of the rise of imperialism and its attempt to unify first Europe then the planet. Then the 2nd International Left in its majority (bar a small minority Bolsheviks, Spartacists, Serbians etc) took sides against the nations its ruling class was at war against voting for war credits. Now the ruling class has gone global the Left has gone anti-national, against its own nation in almost every single country. Syriza is no exception to this but in reality one of the most vociferous proponents of it. It is setting itself up as the saviour of 'Europe'. There is no Europe but an agglomeration of imperialist and capitalist nation states which are on a course of merging, but as they aren't all of the same economic and developmental level and as a series of core countries started the initial process off then their interests would be paramount. As such we see what is happening to Greece predicted eloquently by the precursors of Syriza in the form of EDA in 1960**(iii)**. It's no coincidence that they go out of their way supporting and promoting all anti-Greek acts (eg by the US 'Macedonian' neighbouring statelet or by FIFA which fines Greek football teams)

Tsipras Shadow Government-Economics Team

The Oxford connection of neo-liberal economists is deep and goes way back.

A relative (nephew) of the Greek civil war General Tsakalotos who was responsible for the civil war in 1946-49 against the Greek communist movement Efklidios Tsakalotos grew up in Holland and London. A close personal friend of Stournaras the current neo-fascist Economics Minister of Greece they had a joint publication regarding Greece and the prospects of it in the EU when they were at Oxford together in 1992. (Greece: On the Road of Economic and Monetary Union Problems and Prospects)

What are their differences? Stournaras asks for the Greek peoples to be erased, which is the aim of the EU's economic genocide programme, whilst Tsakalotos asks for Germany's surpluses to be spent in a manner he sees fit (naturally in the mass importation of immigrant labour which is always the priority of neoliberal economists) just in case Greek workers attempt to raise their heads once more in the future. Just like Mbeki became known as the South African Thatcherite so Tsakalotos having the same experience as Mbeki of living in Thatcherite Britain and in particular when his wife Heather Gibson is a bankster and a close collaborator of the central bankster of Greece Provopoulos (sources newspost gr).

Alongside Stournaras both Tsakalotos are responsible for the publications below: Investment and Credit Rationing in Four European Economies), as και το 2001 (The Changing Role on Finance in Southern European European Economies: Will There be an improvement in Economic Performance.

So how does one explain the various interconnected relationships between what goes for the **fake Left and banking circles?** Not that this is the only one. Antarsya's main component the split Socialist Workers Party of Greece whose main leader was Panos Garganas has a brother who was the central bankster of Greece for a decade or more overseeing the entry of Greece into the EU under the neo-liberal Simitis regime. One doesn't normally assume a brother is linked to a brother politically, but two cornerstone principles of the EU *'the freedom of movement of capital and labour'* are expressed directly by the two brothers, one a bankster, the other a 'revolutionary' (never known to have done a day's paid work since graduating from the USA).

The explanation is quite simple. There is no organised Left. Like during WW1 the majority became part of the system voting for war credits so in our time the economic war inaugurated by the collapse of American capitalism after the outbreak of the banking crises of 2007/8 has meant they are just part of the social system they allege to dispute. They spent the latter part of the 2000 decade defending globalisation and its most direct feature in European societies: the mass importation of labour and now they will be in leading roles in defending promoting and extending the collapse of capitalism into society.

It's no coincidence the closer they get to state power we hear statements like the following that, 'only 5% of the debt is odious' in other words 95% has been made by MP Stamatis from Syriza in their radio station Kokkino 105.5

Charity replaces politics under the guise of 'Solidarity for All'

 **Social Medicine Centre for Solidarity**

As a response to (GD's known charity interventions of providing food to hungry Greeks) Syriza inaugurated 'solidarity for all'. If the role of the Left was to provide charity to collapsing capitalism then it should join the Church. Charity can exist as a form of resistance to capitals onslaught, in other words forms of self-rule by providing much needed skills in a deteriorating situation eg. how to reconnect electricity once cut off for the banksters taxes, how to organise against repossessions, how to organise people to fight the teargas wielding riot police etc. Reformism in the era of austerity is dead. Capitalism has nothing to give. Hence Syrizas 'charity' aims to support the neo-liberal agenda. They defend the banning of GD (in handing out food in squares, in receiving state subsidies like Syriza does etc.) in other words whilst aiming to ape others they adopt the central core of the neofascist 4th Reich. Turn Greece into a nation of beggars then aim to provide 19th century charity without even asking from their MP's to take the average salary not a multiple of five from it. People who are going hungry now see them as just another bunch of politicians on the make and on the take but for the 'new period'. It's no coincidence that the word MP in Greece which is 'vouleftis' has become 'voleftis' in a word play, meaning 'taker'...

Social layer of Syriza MP's... nouveau riche neo-liberals in disguise

The information below is taken from this site presumably they have followed what is declared in Parliament. This does not imply one cannot have property or savings but the scale of both is illuminating and as always as with all bourgeois parliamentary declarations it isn't what you have but how you got it and information regarding this does not exist anywhere.

If one collects the 71 Syriza MP's we can see that we can build a small city. On paper the poorest is Tsipras but we all know this is just electioneering whereby they ensure he owns nothing on paper, like the KKE's ex-General Secretary Papariga (but she does receive a Euro 40k pension despite the average in Greece being Euro 7k). Here are a few examples...

-Panagiotis Kouroumblis owns according to data from the parliamentary offices 18 buildings, 9 warehouses, 4 garages, 3 cars etc ex-PASOK

-Dimitris Stratoulis hasn't paid the council tax despite owning 19 properties

-Nikolas Voutsis 12 buildings 7 of which are in the rich northern suburb of Athens Kifisia, was the main editor of EKON Rigas Fereos (youth wing of the Euros in the 1980's). His son was involved in bank robberies not out of need but out of ideological convictions… as he wanted to show 'his opposition to the banking system' stated in April 2008 by George Vogiatzis

-Valavani Olga Nandia 15 properties, E800k abroad 3 cars
- Rena Dourou 9 properties (ex-PASOK now Syriza MP who had water thrown on her by Kasidiaris GD MP)

-Dimitris Papadimoulis 11 properties E500k in cash more than E500k in shares
-Dragasakis -6 properties E150k

-Alexis Mitropoulos 12 Properties
http://pisoapothnkoyrtina.blogspot.gr/2013/12/blog-post_7090.html

PASOK & ND both together and both separately via the media outlets aligned with them which are part of the actual state system as they get most of the public works projects assigned to them by politicians have created an aura of this deeply 'radical left party' which has no social base in society as a whole, has limited support in society apart from electoral and its politics from its leading cadres are ultra-conservative. In the early 90's Synaspismos used to go round carrying Greek flags. When the tide of mass unlimited illegal immigration started they dropped all symbols of Greece and adopted… red flags. They were the organisation that pioneered the move away from all 'communist' symbols and became famous for engaging every foreign power in anti-Greek positions. Everyone had 'rights' but not for Greeks. Soon they will be faced in defending Greek people's rights against the claims of foreign banksters like those that own the National Bank of Greece. The mask then will fall.

Foreign Policy and NATO

When the Americans due to their involvement alongside Germany in the destruction and collapse of ex-Yugoslavia (for decades a global leader of the non-aligned states) started to set up military bases and offload tonnes of fiat currency by setting up dependent statelets like FYROM, Syriza youth campaigned against the 'chauvinism' of the Greek populace which demonstrated in their hundreds of thousands against the demands by the 'macedonian' statelet. A core component of ultra-globalist demands originated from OSE (Greek state caps) who split and half their organisation went into Syriza. They campaigned across a series of 'rights' for every anti-Greek demand, by Turkey, by Skopje, by mass illegal immigrants under the pseudo rights of 'no borders' that the 'Aegean belongs to its fishes' and their views are quite widespread in Syriza.

It's no coincidence then that Syriza MP Dourou is in the foreign policy department of Syriza and she was in the previous PASOK administration. Her 'left' profile was raised by the media via water being thrown at her by a GD MP Kasidiaris. In Tsipras speech at the Brookings Institute in the USA (he obviously can't go to Bilderberg so openly as his cover will be blown he stated the following:

"I heard the person who spoke before me saying that I represent the radical left [the English translation of his party's name] … But how are we really radical? Those who engage in scare-mongering will tell you that our party will come to power, rip up our agreements with the European Union and the IMF, take our country out of the euro zone, break off all of Greece's ties with the cultured—with the civilized West, and then turn Greece into a new North Korea."

http://www.wsws.org/en/articles/2013/01/26/tsip-j26.html

'Odious' Debt or Real Debt? – Flipflopping Syriza

Most people assume that Syriza will cancel the debt if in power immediately or they wont stick to the budget of the previous administration in Brussels.

Let's look at how the argument in Syriza has developed from Tsoukalatos,

"The debt default and euro exit option was adopted by a wide range of nationalistic forces whose anti-imperialist doctrine rhetoric was not always easily distinguishable from that of certain sections of the Left. The nationalistic currents mobilised around such slogans as **'Greece does not owe anything, it is owed'** *and* **'end the foreign occupation'** *both statements that resonate powerfully in a country that has not forgotten its wartime experience and all that followed. But this line of reasoning does not allow for any internal division between the 'people' and the 'nation'." P138-39*

When they all governed together in 1989-90 KKE (Sinaspismos pre-Syriza) New Democracy and PASOK...

Τόκοι - Χρεολύσια (προϋπολογισμός 2012)	
Δαπάνες για καταπτώσεις εγγυήσεων	1,623
Τόκοι και λοιπές δαπάνες δημοσίου χρέους	12.750
Χρεολύσια μεσομακροπρόθεσμου δανεισμού	41,900
Χρεολύσια βραχυπρόθεσμου δανεισμού	25.000
Υποχρεώσεις φορέων γενικής κυβέρνησης	6,000
Δαπάνες εξυπηρέτησης δημόσιας πίστης	215
Δαπάνες εξυπηρέτησης εξοπλιστικών προγραμ.	1,000
Σύνολο	88,488

1) Τα ποσά είναι σε δισ. ευρώ.
2) Πηγή: Πίνακας 3.9 του Κρατικού Προϋπολογισμού 2012, σελ. 57

From the national budget in 2012. Just in one year E88billion has been assigned to interest payments.

Over a 30 year period the amount becomes astronomical taking into account the overall debt continues to become larger and larger. Not long ago it was announced with much fanfare that Greece repaid a debt taken out in the 19th century. So unless a conference is held to ascertain what the debt is and how much of it is real all repayments should stop immediately. This was the original position of Syriza when it was the party of 4%. Now it has grown its position keeps on changing. Tsoukalatos expresses the desire of the ruling elite in Tsipras close circle to *both repay the debt and get a rescheduling* by essentially following the Soros line that 'Germany is repeating what France did at the end of WW1' ie with its punitative payments against Greece it will bankrupt the EU.

It's no coincidence that Glezos who for years was in PASOK and is the living embodiment of Greek resistance to German occupation is also head of the Committee for WW2 reparations against Germany and this might imply he is there as a show, to ensure the new turn of Syriza in accepting the debt repayments has his blessing. But in all the charade the issue at stake is that people don't have money to pay for these interest payments anymore. They are odious, corrupt and belong to the shadow banking system for they aren't out in the open in a clear and transparent way

Εξέλιξη δαπανών εξυπηρέτησης δημόσιου χρέους 1981-2010

Έτος	Έσοδα	Χρεολύσια	%	Τόκοι	%	Σύνολο	%
1981	1 142	57	5.0	183	16.0	240	21.0
1982	1 614	64	3.9	199	12.3	263	16.3
1983	1 992	70	3.5	308	15.4	377	18.9
1984	2 468	124	5.0	401	16.3	526	24.3
1985	3 000	195	6.5	725	23.3	900	29.8
1986	3 660	381	10.0	837	21.7	1 220	32.7
1987	5 740	756	13.3	1 187	20.9	1 943	34.2
1988	6 345	446	9.3	1 611	30.1	2 057	38.5
1989	5 797	603	10.4	1 850	32.0	2 453	42.4
1990	7 020	994	12.6	3 413	43.1	4 407	55.6
1991	9 987	2 704	21.0	4 203	42.1	6 907	69.2
1992	12 406	6 406	52.0	4 122	34.0	10 528	87.6
1993	15 341	4 707	35.0	6 228	43.7	10 935	82.0
1994	18 376	7 172	48.0	8 000	57.0	16 082	104.6
1995	17 469	7 000	42.8	9 300	51.8	16 984	98.8
1996	18 416	10 286	65.7	9 600	52.4	19 896	108.1
1997	20 807	10 169	45.6	9 000	59.5	19 955	95.0
1998	25 209	9 000	38.4	9 079	35.2	18 701	74.2
1999	29 000	6 291	21.9	9 254	32.0	16 542	69.0
2000	32 000	13 132	41.0	9 498	29.7	22 633	70.7
2001	33 000	11 610	36.2	9 200	26.1	20 907	63.3
2002	34 079	20 280	59.5	9 538	25.0	29 818	84.6
2003	36 621	20 783	56.3	9 208	28.0	29 077	81.3
2004	39 474	18 444	46.7	8 798	23.3	27 842	70.0
2005	42 083	20 378	48.4	9 508	22.6	29 886	71.0
2006	44 921	16 699	36.8	10 349	23.0	26 938	60.7
2007	48 465	22 195	45.9	9 582	19.6	31 776	65.7
2008	51 095	26 246	51.4	11 052	21.5	37 298	73.0
2009	49 724	29 035	58.5	12 145	24.4	41 260	83.0
2010	51 942	19 560	37.7	12 620	24.7	32 360	62.0

| Σύνολα | 2009 3 460 | | 48.6 | 190 220 | 26.9 | 480 470 | 72.3 |

Πηγή: Κρατικός προϋπολογισμός

A graph showing that Greece paid E480 billion from 1981 to 2010 in interest payments alone.

According to N Bogiopoulos the one time star journalist of the KKE, Greece has paid around E1trillion in interest payments in a tv show with the journalist Hatzinikolaou, much larger than what is presented above and as with all government statistics they are probably below one third of what they show.

Tsoukalatos goes on to criticise another member of Syriza, Kouvelakis with the following snipe,

"Syrizas stance with respect to the exit strategy had nothing to do with seeking a role of passive repositories for popular rage' Kouvelakis 2011) but more with a class analysis of the capitalist crisis and a historical understanding of the dynamics and dangers of nationalist politics'" p.138-139

Despite being a bourgeois trained economist Tsoukalatos shows a total disregard of even basic Marxism in the realms of economics. His whole book talks about Greece as if it is an equal member of the EU not a dependant state. This is in direct contrast with the traditional position of the Left which always considered Greece to be a dependent state which needed to be developed ie industrialised and reach an imperialist stage of capitalism. His diatribes against 'nationalism' are a cover to support, defend and promote 'good' globalisation as opposed to bad 'neo-liberal' one, in other words the mythical period in the mid-1990s when he was co-authoring books with Stournaras the current genocidal finance Minister of Greece. Such is the farce that if anyone was truly concerned they would have asked for his expulsion after the scandal erupted that he personally owned shares in Black Rock one of the investors Skouries gold mines in Northern Greece.

On GD and ...'neo-nazism'

Just as the economic analysis of the state of Greek capitalism is geared in such a manner where it begins and ends with EU participation so the analysis of the growth of neo-nazism in Greece is short of any Marxist analysis **(v).** Having adopted the global corporate media interest in showing who a bunch of amateurs who are followers of the American backed junta of the 60's went from 0.29% to 8% and now hover anywhere between 10-20% whilst the KKE is trying to get more than 3% electorally are truly a neo-nazi party with imperialist appetites ie about to march on the EU and take control by first purifying Greece from its non-indigenous elements (as shown by the example of overturning a few tables of immigrants in a market in Rafina).

In reality this is about supporting the current neo-fascist Junta that runs Greece, on Executive Decrees, has suspended habeus corpus, has passed laws allowing banks to freeze bank accounts, shuts down big public sector concerns overnight and provides zero to the mass unemployment they have presided over. For over a decade a cross section of Antarsya supporters and Syriza ones have focused almost exclusively on Golden Dawn, *not the explosive issue of mass unlimited immigration*, to the extent that they go round cracking heads open in poor communities which they label all as being 'racist' and 'fascist' not wanting their areas to be turned into third world dumping grounds. Just as Tsipras requires Lafazani to acquire 'radical left' credentials so Syriza as a whole requires Golden Dawn to acquire 'left wing' credentials as if they are re-fighting the Greek civil war. The same people who handed over their weapons in 1944 on orders from Stalin thus aiding reaction and the quisling formations that collaborated with Hitler. It's no coincidence that the same families or descendants of this Occupation are now still calling the shots in the new economic occupation of Greece by the foreign banksters. *Plus ça change, plus c'est la même chose.*

It's also absurd to vote for the banning of the state subsidy against GD and to openly support police-state measures and the banning of the party, for this only increases its support in society as a whole and further fits in with the political profile created by Samaras himself of right wing extremism and left wing extremism whilst the ruling junta are of course the arbiters of the 'constitutional order' and 'democracy' itself. A democracy which if it doesn't kill you from mass unemployment will almost certainly wipe you out via the tax system. Syriza's pseudo humanitarian concerns regarding illegal immigration can only be judged by the yardstick of their concerns to their own nation which is clearly wanting. It resembles in a refracted form the 'humanitarian concerns' of western imperialism in the Balkans when they were 'liberating' areas by bombing them to smithereens. Those who allege that mass immigration is above classes and can only be viewed from a fake humanitarian perspective have obviously forgotten a core principle of Marx in economics. Any oversupply of labour leads inevitably collapsed wages. When one by one all the old labour unions of Greece were decimated with the contribution of the political union leaderships aligned with Syriza, the labour movement was decapitated. Syriza is a by product of this decapitation, which it contributed to.

Insofar as the Warsaw Pact and the old Soviet Union existed professional western leftists had a role model they could look up to and promote as being an alternative, both from the point of view of limited unemployment and a stable standard of living that provided the basics, housing, healthcare and education. That role model is long gone and their new role model is the USA and not any USA in any particular period of history (for instance LB Johnsons Great Society reforms) but Obamas USA which has pretended 'growth' has returned on the backs of QE and minimum wage jobs, which need to be supplemented with food stamps (around 50m on the programme now!). Hence the fact that within the Greater Athens region (Attiki) Syriza came first in the last elections (21012) and GD second for all those voters under 50 years of age shows that the electoral base of both parties aren't in reality organised forces they just want the same things from a different perspective and this will be the thorny issue for Syriza: how to satisfy demands by Greeks for a basic standards of living whilst at the same time satisfying the demands of the planet 'for freedom of movement' and relocation to wherever they see fit? GD has already announced it will rename itself if banned, so to support state bans without defeating the root causes that lead to the growth of such political bandits (supporters of the American backed junta) actually serves the opposite purpose than those intended.

What follows are eye-witness reports of the first 18months of Syriza in opposition and documents from history (Pouliopoulos, EDA) covering the issues of the present through the prism of the past, articles submitted to the CAFÉ (Campaign Against Federalism in Europe) **(vi)** and NO2EU tradeunion information group **(vii)** as well as a timely contribution by T Fotopoulos **(viii)** (regarding the crisis of the Left. Included as well is information regarding Greece's role in the EU from Bogiopoulos (one time journalist star of the KKE) **(ix)** and also on the Drachma written during the heady days of street protests in the squares of Athens in 2011 which originates from another book by the same author *'How the IMF Broke Greece and the Role of the Fake Left'*.

What follows next: **Default or Accommodation to the EU-Banksters**, we await to see in practice, not words. An economy that has been devastated by the entrance into the EU confirms the old adage that necessity becomes the mother of invention and the Greek nation will require to take drastic action if it wants to survive and not be erased by the New World Order. By restoring hope in a society in decline with a programme of growth based, on the productive re-development of society with new cleaner forms of energy, a reorganisation of production to meet need, not profit, with the aim of creating a Balkan Federation to destroy the destructive power of imperialism. An imperialism which has devastated this region in the last century with constant wars, coups, economic collapses, population transfers and now the all pervasive stench of gross corruption by a ruling class which belongs to the dustbin of history.

VN Gelis

10th February 2014

2 SYRIZA EYE-WITNESS REPORTS
JUNE-DEC 2012

June 2012

Syriza's Athens Electoral Public Meeting-Omonia Square

Known as the United Social Front the platform was at the bottom quarter of the square overlooking the two 4x hotels that have shut down in the last two years. It was organised in such a manner to show large crowds. Only a few years ago the whole square could be filled up and the platform would be in the middle of it.

Now no party and in particular one that hovered around 4% can fill squares. People have lost faith in organised politics as it is organised as it has become fashionable to say one thing prior to elections and do the exact opposite when in power. There must have been around 25k. For a party which received 1.1 million votes and is poised to receive more, there are no electoral offices that have been rented and there is no actual organised increase in membership, proportionate to the rise in electoral support.

First up was Sofia Sakorafa who read her speech in a calm but wooden manner representing those essentially that have left PASOK, who have grown in the last period, ranging from union bureaucrats to alleged close collaborators of PASOK (images have appeared in the press that Dourou who had water thrown at her by GD in a tv panel talk show, was a close collaborator of the imprisoned ex-Defence Minister of the Siemens scandal Akis Tzohatsopoulos.

In the crowds one could discern all the different groups that make up Syriza, KOE, Xekinima, Marxistiki Foni (last two were in PASOK for over twenty years-Grantites) DEA (ex-SWP who voted for PASOK for as long as they were independent). They have all found a home in the most Europhile party of the Left assuming a new era is dawning where we can have reformist parties in an era when reformism is dead.

But they are there only because Tsipras appeared on the stage and gave an unscripted speech which essentially was focused on the message of unity and that this is the time for the Left. Enough damage has been done enough destruction and that if the current economic policy continues the Eurozone will break apart. The era of corruption is over and we need to get Greece back to work. Terrorise the terrorists he stated. Compared to all else Tsipras can hold his own but the content is lacking.

Only one in five Greeks who are officially unemployed get any benefit whatsoever of 361 euros per month and the tax bills issued this month to all have essentially dropped wages and pensions by another one or two monthly amounts. Most wages are now around E1k (less than UK's minimum wage) in the public sector and the economics of depression don't seem to change as capitalism is collapsing and no amount of manoeuvring within the present socio-economic system will change that. Things are about to get a lot worse.

If Syriza assumes power the Europhiles will pre-dominate and try to do everything in their power to defend the Eurozone and go against its left wing and its own electoral base. To what extent they will be successfull will depend on a variety of factors. One is that they are united prior to assuming power. Once in power the internal faction divisions will come to the fore. That is why Syriza doesn't want to win outright and wants to govern with others. The rotteness of the far 'left' grouplets is about to be magnified for all to see.

Democratic Left in Power-(Syrizas ex-cdes in Sinaspismos) Kouvelis

In what are disgusting scenes the forces of the fake left in Greece have entered a new stage in their despicable alliance with the IMF inside and outside Parliament in destroying workers conditions.

The 9th month strike of the Steelworkers of Manesis factory on the outskirts of Athens has been broken by the intervenion of a Public Prosecutor who deemed the strike illegal and ordered the police to break up the picket line and open it up. The Democratic Left has key appointments in the Ministry of Labour and they oversaw this process. Until only recently they were one of the factions that made up Syriza. Now they are implementing the pro-Maastricht policies they all jointly voted for in 1992.

KKE Sellouts

Having kept the strike isolated and going on for 9 months whose purpose is to sap and destroy the energy of the workers there so they split and demand their 'return to work' which a few did, thus provoking the latest attempt at breaking the strike, the KKE is now calling for the rest of the labour movement to defend the sacked steelworkers. For over two years alongside the Greek TUC-GSEE they have supported the maximum of 48hour strikes and always marching on their own and inventing a new area to disperse, around

Akropolis. Here though we have the KKE acting allegedly in ultra-militant fashion supporting an 'indefinite strike'. But is it thus?

As Manesis has more than one factory and as the main cause of the strike was the attempt to impose a 4hour day and maximum E450 a month salaray, the factory in Athens which employed predominantly Greeks walked out. They attempted a few times to shut down the factory in Volos (which employs 'class brothers' as the KKE now openly refers to illegal immigrant scabs) in such a manner where the controlled the events and ensured there was no conflict, ie allowing the police to run the show and they being a second line of police against the strikers. This local policy is reflected on a national level when they sent all their organised forces early one morning to defend Parliament as the second wave of IMF cuts were going through back in October 2011.

Having failed to shut down the Volos factory they continued with the Athens strike up until workers there would be fed up. By allowing the factory in Volos to continue Manesis increased his production and covered a section of the losses of production in Athens. This was well known. The emphasis therefore should have been to shut that factory down at all costs. The only strike that is illegal is one that loses. Having divided the workforce they had a golden opportuinity this week to occupy the factory, thus forcing the riot police to storm them out. When another factory in Thessalonika was occupied the KKE refuse to follow this direct action path. Instead they were 'caught off guard' and riot police broke the small picket line at 5a am on 20th July.

One must take into account the KKE's fake left workers slogan 'Worker nothing turns without your Hands' didn't obviously apply to this concrete situation. Why didn't they occupy the factory? They would have been confronted with running it, being taken to court by they owner, so they preferred now to be on the outside looking in.

On 20th July then called for an early lunchtime demo and another the following day in the afternoon. The demos were timed thus that they were over before they started, and the main thoroughfare wasn't closed. They don't want workers discussing any different strategy than theirs nor do they want to win this strike. Around 5,000 people turned up to the demos.

They have now called for the rest of the labour movement to participate and Syriza has said they will support the demo in central Athens on the issue for the following Monday. The government is producing propaganda showing that Syriza-KKE-Golden Dawn all support the strikes as they have spoken at their meetings or handed food parcels to them, under the explanation that the government wants people to get back to work whilst they want people unemployed...

An Undeclared Popular Front.

With the Democratic Left in the Greek Labour Ministry the IMF led government continues apace in its rapacious attacks against Greek workes in an unscripted alliance with those who aren't in government Syriza-KKE. This strike is a precursor of things to come when the wholescale privatisation of the public sector starts which Kouvelis stated would happen post-haste by Xmas.

KKE members defending the IMF controlled Parliament

December 2012

Syriza 6th Months in Opposition: The troikas Last Card?

"I like Tsipras. He has something fresh to offer. He has achieved much in the role of official opposition..."

Kostas Karamanlis New Democracy ex- Premier to Vima
24th February 2013

Despite announcing last June, to much fanfare, that this was the last Saturday before a new anti-Monetary Union dawn, Tsipras has presided over six months in opposition. In those six months we have seen the future role for Syriza in action.

They are *ECB- IMF appendages in waiting*: they are the Dem Left's successors; Maastricht's honourable heirs. Tsipras flip flops on a range of issues: accepting NATO; accepting a rescheduling of the debts rather than demanding their immediate cancellation; asking people to stay on the streets whilst being the first to depart; selling out strikes etc. This has set the tone for what a possible future Syriza government could look like, assuming an open dictatorship isn't declared or a peoples' rebellion occurs.

In 2012 Syriza grew from 4% electoral support to 27%. This was the shortest period of time in history, and happened because of the response by Greeks to the international blackmail and global corporate media attack that they are the 'laziest' 'most corrupt' 'biggest shirker' nation on Earth. They refused to prop up bankrupt and corrupt Western banks. But it was due primarily to the fact that opposition to 'Grexit' (Greek exit from the Eurozone) no longer held sway with a majority of the electorate. The 40% that didn't vote in the election knew they were all the same anyway and kept their conscience clean. But for those who did, the last six months have been the biggest disappointment in an opposition, possibly ever in Greek history.

Tsipras at the Karamanlis foundation function with Samaras, Papoulias and other 4th Reich Quislings

The economic genocide continues apace. There are daily suicides. There are more than 450,000 families with no breadwinner (in total 1.3 million people). There is around 30% official unemployment. Probably around 50% of the population are underemployed; wages have lost around 40-50% of their value. Hospitals have ceased to function in any meaningful sense. We are in **an economic tsunami akin to the period of war rationing**. Within this monstrous situation, which shows no signs of abating the opposition parties (Syriza, KKE, Independent Greeks etc.) have done nothing apart from engaging in *waffle* from the sidelines, or turned out to make funeral orations after the defeat of strikes **led** by them: Steelworkers (KKE), Metroworkers (Antarsya), Sailors (Syriza). They drone on about how in the next life, we will win, but in this one we can only endure *defeat after defeat.*

Coordinated campaigns of disorganised resistance and disunity are their hallmarks. They should register a patent and see if they can continue to make money on it, for that is all they are concerned about: receiving their state subsidies as official parties; MP's sinecures; pension deals as union presidents, who, if they serve just one term, are pensioned off and so on).

It was the people in their hundreds of thousands who saw off Papandreou in June-July and again in October 2011 via mass occupations of squares and disruption of annual military parades. They reduced his party PASOK to a rump with a rabble rouser, Venizelos, whose nickname is Benito, in charge. PASOK's only lament is that Golden Dawn took votes from them. It appears once more that it will be the people who will get rid of the latest Tripartite Quisling formation known in Greece as the Internal Troika. They gave 1 in 3 of their votes to Syriza and what have they got in return?

Syriza's Abysmal role in 'Opposition'

The initial elation by Tsipras and Stamoulis arising from their not winning the election suggested the possibility that they agreed not to win. Was there an electronic cooking of the books? After all, the company that computes the results is owned by Latsis and Vgenopoulos, ship owners par excellence. With this they would be able to *'rock the government in... legality'*. In other words they would be a pliant opposition.

Meeting Shimon Perez

Tsipras' first big foray in Opposition was to state we will not go back to the Drachma and met with Shimon Perez ex-Premier of the Zionist US airbase going by the name of Israel. This was to guarantee that any oil exploration projects, as was also the case with his friends in the Cypriot Government, would be handed to Israeli companies and that any future president would guarantee their investments.

Hiding from the anti-Merkel anti-MoU (EU Monetary Union) protests

During Merkel's visits, despite ex-PASOK MP's Sakorafa stating that we will stay on the streets so as to end the third round of cuts imposed by the MoU, what did they do? They left Parliament and held their banner outside the steps whilst the rest of the population routinely were teargassed. Despite union members dressing up in SS uniforms and chanting '*down with the 4th Reich!*', Syriza refused to leave the Parliament, stating that to do so would go against Parliamentary democracy. When hundreds of thousands demonstrate and the desire and need is for them to stay out to win, if there was even a nominal leadership this could be achieved. Instead we have a commitment to Parliamentarism which is beyond even what the parliamentarians are doing. After all, they no longer govern via Parliament, which governs by **Executive Decree,** signed and sealed by a corrupt President whose nickname in street protests is Papoulia-Julia (porn actress deliberately made famous by the corporate media during the arrival of the IMF so as to confuse sections of the population).

Avoiding all slum visits in Brazil and flipflopping on debt repayments in Argentina

We then had Tsipras' long holidays to Latin America to gain international kudos as if the big boys across the Atlantic aren't supporting him as the next best hope for their financial sharks who want their pound of flesh from the decapitated Greek nation. Brazil was touted as a model of development, the country that not too long ago was bumping off street kids and has a police force, which to this day, makes the Greek one look like it operates in the spirit of Gandhi.

Tsipras in Brazil, with sunglasses for a visit!

In Argentina, the country survived its economic collapse only after an insurrection, the collapse of many governments and the restoration of the Peso, decoupled from the US Dollar. But despite Tsipras knowing all this, all we heard from him back in Greece was how they paid back a portion of their debts and…restructured them.

Brookings Institute and Washington, Tsipras Made in the USA

Tsipras pro-American stance started to reveal itself just six months after being the main opposition. Whilst not still able to go openly to the inauguration of a US President, he was there soon after speaking in one of the most Cold-War institutes in the USA, the Brookings Institute. He said nothing less than that austerity is killing capitalism and he wanted to save it. According to the German media, one of the meetings in New York was funded by Soros, that well known financier who always seeks his pound of flesh against nations when he isn't actively destabilizing them culturally.

Metro workers burning back to work papers...

The message back in Greece, in particular after Syriza's conference in early December, was that there are two wings in the party: the 'pragmatist' wing that sees Obama as a saviour and the 'left' party wing led by Lafazani, which oscillates from saying that it wants the return of a national currency, to talking up strikes in order to aid in their betrayal when the government announces another 'emergency decree' to ban them.

Tsipras flipflopped on being against NATO, considering it no longer is an issue under the present dire economic circumstances, despite the fact that, according to bourgeois commentators such as the Guardian's Helena Smith, Greece probably spent around 250 Billion Euros in arms. Tsipras implies he wants to maintain these payments at all costs, along with Greece's external commitments, including soldiers as part of NATO, in Kosovo, Afghanistan etc - and wherever else NATO decides to invade in the future (even Greece itself if it comes to it!)

Politicians don't run Greece, neither does Parliament. So don't expect anything from the Fake Left either.

With the Troika in charge of every Ministry; with some banks being funded by the ECB; with no National Agricultural Bank; with all decisions regarding 'national' economic policy set by Brussels, then

Greece is no longer a state with its own decision making bodies. It has become an **EU Protectorate**. The fake left refuses to accept this vital fact in order to maintain its role, which is none other than propping up the IMF. It does so by its policy of coordinated disunited resistance, allowing section after section of employees to be dragged into defeat, kicking and screaming.

Whilst Metro workers and Sailors tore up their militaristic orders from the government to return to work, the union tops brought out lawyers who threatened them with being fired, arguing on the picket line for them to go home. Then we had the despicable spectacle of the fake 'lefts' appearing to march back in defeat and give militant sounding speeches about the future 'struggle'. Lafazanis and Papariga turned up in unison for the sellout, whilst everywhere else they march separately, here they struck together!

Greeks waiting for free handouts from Greek farmers

The mass privatisation and selloffs of Greece will be stopped only by popular struggle, as occurred in Keratea over the creation of dumpsites right next to peoples' homes. Whether we get a new government in the coming period (Syriza in power with Ind Greeks seems most likely as the KKE is refusing to join Syriza) this kind of resistance will continue because the present government seems to now be a busted flush.

Samaras' handing over sea rights to Turkey, wanting to seel the main state owned Greek gas import company to the Americans, despite being offered double by the Russians have all contributed to this inherent national bankruptcy of the internal Troika.

The hundred thousand who marched for the umpteenth time in another 24 hour General Strike in Athens on Wednesday 20th February shows that people are willing to take on the IMF. All that is lacking is the leadership.

Updates:

25.02.13

Syrizas economics team around Dragasakis announced that due to budgetary constraints and the delay in assuming power it will probably be impossible the longer Syriza remains out of power or constitutes the backbone of a new government to restore the minimum wage as promised to the pre-Troika period.

26.02.13

Tsipras is to speak at the 15year funeral oration for the founder of New Democracy Konstantinos Karamanlis. From marching with PASOK-Dimar now speaking at New Democracy functions....

03.03.13

Alavanos ex-leader of Sinaspismos wants to found the Party of the Drachma in discussion talks with Antarsya...Kazakis of EPAM...

Three Stooges in Govt Samaras, Kouvelis, Venizelos

January 2013

3. Golden Dawn and Pseudo anti-fascism in the service of the Troika

Fake Left Marching with Troika. Fascist 'anti-fascism'? ...

POE-OTA union mobilisation against the representative of the EU-4th Reich Project Chancellor Merkel in Greece

Leon Trotsky bitterly denounced **"the empty abstraction of anti-fascism"** and the Popular Front in his writings on Spain as follows: **"The very concepts of 'anti-fascism' and 'anti-fascist' are fictions and lies. Marxism approaches all phenomena from a class standpoint. [Republican prime minister] Azaña is 'anti-fascist' only to the extent that fascism hinders bourgeois intellectuals from carving out parliamentary or other careers. Confronted with the necessity of choosing between fascism and the proletarian revolution, Azaña will always prove to be on the side of the fascists. His entire policy during the seven years of revolution proves this."**

What are the real reasons behind the hue and cry against Golden Dawn?
There is an international effort by the British media (e.g. Paul Mason on Newsnight), the Greek corporate media (Lambrakis media), Reuters, the US media (New York Times) and a whole host of organisations the world over who are embedded to the agenda of the corporate New World Order. This is the same corporate media that sold the lies of Al Quaeda and Weapons of Mass Destruction to launch the 'War on Terror' i.e. the neo-colonialist brutal occupation of both Afghanistan and Iraq on behalf of the oil and drug cartels that are part of the clique that rules the world.

In the piece below:
http://greecesolidarity.org/?p=410
"Love or nothing: The real Greek parallel with Weimar
Paul Mason, who originates from the 'Far' Left, asserts the following:
"Of all the operas written during Germany's Weimar Republic (1919-33), probably the most haunting is the last.
Kurt Weill's The Silver Lake, written with playwright Georg Kaiser, tells the story of two losers – a good-hearted provincial cop and the thief he has shot and wounded – as they make their way through a society ruined by unemployment, corruption and vice. After spending a week again in Greece – amid riots, hunger and far right violence – I finally understood it."

When in reality if one is to use culture to be appropriate for Greece one would have to use Brecht or more appropriately his last play written in 1929 'St Joan of the Slaugherhouse' which depicts the collapse of capitalism. History does not repeat itself in a linear fashion. Stalinism and fascism aren't coming back in the same form. They are dead.

Searching for historical parallels and from them issuing statements about Greece, which not so long ago was characterised as having 'humane capitalism' but now it resembles Weimar Germany. This serves certain New World Order agendas, which is what Paul Mason's role is.

After all he is on a lecture circuit for personal gain and promotion selling the story in his latest book, that global capitalism is suffering a new 1848!

No to the 4th Reich

The rise and rise of Golden Dawn...

Golden Dawn, whose precursor was EPEN which received 7% in 1977, are supporters of foreign backed military juntas and have constantly revealed this. They are embedded rightists who have supported the foreign backed juntas. In that sense they differ not one iota from the internal troika running Greece now. There never was a neo-nazi movement in Greece for it cannot have mass social support as Greece never was a developed imperialist state. This myth of the developed imperialist nature of Greece is peddled by those who are supporters and promoters of the cornerstones of EU free trade policies (in labour, capital and goods). The organisations that make up Syriza were either embedded PASOKites all their life or were supporters of Maastricht, ex-KKE who had no moral issue governing with New Democracy and PASOK in 1989 and 1990.

On Saturday 6th December 2012 a demonstration **organised by the Town Halls** allegedly against 'fascism' occurred. Official participants in this demo was Kaminis (Athens Mayor), Vallianatos (head of the Homosexual Association of Greece), Manos (ex-New Democracy extreme free marketer who called the arrival of immigrants a blessing for capitalism), Tzimeros (extreme free marketer), PASOK MP's, Dimar, Syriza and Antarsya alongside Amnesty International and other US based NGO's. We have had a Troika government for more than 2 ½ years; now an internal Troika (ND, PASOK, Dimar) are presiding over around 30% unemployment which shows no sign of abating and over 3,500 suicides without including those who have had heart attacks or diagnosed with a severe disease due to the economic crash (lack of medicines and hospital care now being a permanent phenomenon).

Instead of the *Left leaving Parliament campaigning on the streets to overthrow this Quisling formation*, they are embedded in a parliamentary perspective which no longer holds water as the Government runs on Administrative Decrees which don't follow due parliamentary process and German gauleiters introduced into every ministry until the end, i.e. till their final dissolution. No one has called for Genocide charges to be laid against the Troika and no one will; instead **they now march with them on the streets** as there is allegedly a greater danger lurking round the corner.

Despite countless localised rebellions against the wave upon wave of illegal immigration, the violent deaths of countless Greeks young and old, nothing is heard or seen in the corrupt Mass Media: only reports of when an illegal immigrant has their forehead scratched or they allege they were sworn at or chased by people professing to be Golden Dawn do come alive. Golden Dawn hasn't held a single national demonstration in Central Athens and neither has Syriza despite the fact that the situation is getting worse daily. What characterises this period, as opposed to the 1930's, **is that today no one wants to govern**, neither the fake far Left nor the fake far Right.

Town Halls vs Dustmens Union POE-OTA

Last summer there was a dustmen's strike against wage reductions and increases in work loads and the government, then under PASOK-Venizelos, **employed illegal immigrants to break the strike**. This is the agenda they want to impose right across the public sector, using the Bolkeinstein directive to permit companies to be set up so they pay e.g. Bulgarian minimum wages in Greece after they have subcontracted everything. Indicative of this is what occurred in Thessaloniki University where cleaning contractors employing Greeks struck for non-payment of contract payments. It lasted over a month. To ensure the viability of the strike, rubbish was allowed to pile up internally and eventually the Mayor Boutaris in Thessaloniki (from the well known winemaking corporation) called in the riot police to break the strike and arrest striking cleaners. **Where was the fake Left?**

But more importantly, the 'silent demo' held in Athens on 6th December was organised by the Town Halls, the same town halls who are in conflict with their own workers in a long drawn out conflict where they want to sub-contract all council services to foreign multinationals, and here one understands why they funded an 'anti-racist' protest in Central Athens and invited all their political supporters the fake far left with representatives from the government.

The class basis of fake 'anti-fascism' is exposed fully here...

How can one claim to be on the far Left and support the imperialist EU project? How can one claim to be on the far Right and support the Euro stand for EU elections etc?

Political analysis has degenerated from one which defines what one is from deeds, not words, to one which defines what one is from words, not deeds. So as Syriza calls itself the party of the 'radical left' it must thus be, so Golden Dawn must be neo-nazi as they printed an edition of their magazine praising Hitler. The so-called communists for decades defended Stalin's gulags and the Greek KKE still does, so moral lectures from those quarters regarding their political positions are far and infrequent. They believe there is an upturn round the corner, that the collapse of capitalism can be arrested if only it changes course; that neo-Keynesianism is the solution to the crisis and that the stale parameters of the past, viewing things in terms of Right and Left, when what we are really confronted with is much worse: the erasure of nations from the map by the twin threat of economic immiserisation and the flooding of labour markets by anyone and everyone from anywhere, a mini-USA, not in times of economic boom, but economic collapse.

Imperialism has been in a state in collapse since the dawn of the 20th century. We had two imperialist world wars, countless of localised wars and, with the advent of the ex-USSR on the scene, the collapse of capitalism was arrested. But the system managed to go global with the fall of the ex-USSR. The world market exists for the production of goods. America became centre of the de facto world capitalist Empire. All other imperialisms were subsumed under it. The contradictions of the global system are now measured within the context of the collapse of US imperialism.

The rise of the EU occurred as a first step towards a world government with a world currency. But, due to the crisis of overproduction, all the old antagonisms covered for a large historical period came to the surface with the collapse of Lehman Bros. No other area could be antagonistic or in competition with the USA. Hence the Euro had to be curtailed. Greece was chosen for that specific role. Socialism or barbarism has resurfaced not in the distant future but immediately. **The economic hitmen of the Troika would make Hitler look like a democrat in peacetime (he provided jobs, albeit many for war production), our lot are the SS in suits.** You won't hear that from the fake left.

The hue and cry over Golden Dawn has class roots. Those remaining on the left are middle class protest groups. Sensing their imminent immiserisation, want the working class to succumb to globalism as the only alternative to social struggles, *to accepting internal colonies and open slave labour*. If anyone questions the process they are to be labelled a 'racist' by these self-styled... 'anti-racists', who have no moral objection to marching with the representatives of the Troika in Athens...

Who wanted a parliamentary career and who blocked their rise into Parliament? ANTARSYA, EEK, KKE(ML), Den Plirono, EPAM, of they aggregated their votes and one would have got at least another 2% for Syriza hence...so their venom is on the rise of the 'far right'... is about them not passing the grade ie being elected as MP's or ensuring the Left wins. Their policies are about 'divide and rule' pure and simple.

GD wouldn't have been known if it wasn't for its position on illegal immigration, or, more importantly for taking part in residents' protests in central Athens against the squatter camps which developed in the centre. In 2009 they received 0.29% votes or around 20,000 votes, in the local council elections; in November 2010 they received 5.29% and Mihaloliakos (leader of GD) was elected on the Athens City Council. A year later they got 6.97% in the May elections of 2012, surpassing the KKE, and a month later 6.92%, forcing the **KKE into 7th place!** Now they state it might become the 3rd party after Syriza and New Democracy. The irony of Greek rightist 'nationalism' is that GD supported the Euro in its inaugural speech in Parliament as the Greek 'people paid dearly for it', they unfurled a 'junta banner' in a meeting in Crete during the celebrations over the fall of the Junta (i.e. the American backed Papadopoulos one) and, like Syriza, they haven't held a single national demonstration and in their internal party briefings they have said members must play it cool waiting for the 7th Memorandum of Understanding-Bailout packages which have led to 50% cuts in wages and about 25% cuts in pensions (we are now on the 3rd) and power will fall on their lap, in other words when 99% of Greeks are destitute they will...take over!

Golden Dawn wanted the arrest and called for those who protested against Merkel to be locked up. So much for their 'anti-MoU' political stance: as clear and militant as that of Syriza, which remains in Parliament to this day, even when, in neighbouring FYROM, the opposition has left after they openly stated there is no point in remaining in Parliament as it runs on Presidential/Executive Decrees i.e. does not allow voting for the passing of laws, exactly like the fake Greek Parliament.

How could the Fake Left justify its politics of Abstention without GD?

Where can we now find Marshall Skobie or the Varkiza sellout to justify the sellout policies of the fake Left? We can't. But we have GD instead, Mihaloliakos and Kasidiaris. Thank God they emerged as it provides a holy cover for the rotten leaderships of the fake left. It restores their fake credibility. **Combined votes would have meant they would have had a majority but they remain disunited so as to not govern**. The current crisis cannot be resolved in a peaceful manner as the effects of the crisis are no longer peaceful. This is what the fake left peddles, reformist nonsense in an era where reforms have long gone. 50% cuts in wages and pensions 70% plus inflation, busting tax rises, mass homelessness and unemployment are the new terrorism, the neo-fascism of the corporate World Order which they defend and support by asking us to remain embedded to the neo-colonial EU project.

They make noises regarding attacks on Syriza MP's, yet, apart from allegations, we haven't seen any. They allege GD has brutalised and killed illegal immigrants, yet many Greeks have died at the hands of illegal immigrants. To name just a few which led to riots: a father on his way to hospital with his pregnant wife was killed by illegal immigrants for a video camera in central Athens; in Patras a young lad was stabbed to death for complaining about noise on the street. **Syriza have never demonstrated against the killing of Greeks by illegal immigrants.** Why? **They support a one sided policy: anyone but Greeks**. Who said the Greek nation has to accept wave after wave of illegal immigration? The Troika 'anti-racists'! The fake Left used to have the slogan '**National Independence and Popular Rule'**. Now they have forgotten the first part as they are interested in the abolition of the nation states, hence they support 'minority' rights on the principle that Greeks have none. Golden Dawn offices were blown up with the aid of lots of ammunition placed there. This could only come from the security services. Who said anything about that explosion? No one apart from GD of course?

Why? Those who seek to use paramilitary methods against GD (demand its ban), taking into account that Greece has had a history of paramilitary activities centred primarily on the Left (under the guise of attacking 'fascism') **are opening the door to attacks on the Left in general.** Why? Only the Left has fought for social change in Greece. No one else. When I say the Left, I mean the thousands imprisoned, chased, hunted, killed, maimed or butchered by local quislings operating for foreign controllers. Greece was the only country never de-nazified, which the foreign powers used and abused in their Cold War pursuits: let's not forget the despicable role of the British Labour Party in the Greek civil war, working in tandem with the Greek quislings of Hitler.

Imperialist Lectures
For a long period of time the quisling fake leftist grouplets in Athens adopted all the lectures from the imperialists of the north, labelling Golden Dawn a neo-nazi outfit, when previously they had assigned this role to LAOS, to Fini, to Lepen, etc. Fini governed in Italy; so did LAOS in Greece. So what happened? Nothing. All the parties of the fake far right who allege they are 'nationalist' are there just to assume some political steam from the far right for internal reasons. Did mass immigration decrease under Fini's participation in government? Did it under LAOS in Greece? Will it under GD? Of course not! Those embedded in capitalism are also embedded in its current transnational pro-globalist nature. So to listen to frequent lectures from those who have a colonial and racist past like the BBC and its correspondents is like listening to Dracula about blood blanks. It's a total joke.

That is why there is no far right or far left anymore. They are just two sides of the same coin. Embedded to the EU nation destroying project of creating internal colonies. We have been here before. It was known as the 3rd Reich. N o wonder they keep silent when Greeks march in Nazi uniforms and in fake tanks (bought by the Town Hall workers POE-OTA union) against **Merkels 4th Reich, the real fascism of our times, the one that governs and is destroying the Greek nation.**

The fake far lefts' covers are being blown. **The fake far rights will soon be blown as well.**

The good old days when Tsipras and Papandreou used to meet on the 'barricades'...

4. COMMITTEE OF STRUGGLE AGAINST HELLENIC GOLD

The impact of tourism on the economy of N E Halkidiki is alleged to be in the region of 15-20% of GDP. This type of economic looting will bring about an immeasurable attack on tourism of the area, and will undermine the quality of life. The mountain area of Kakkavos supplies the whole region with water. El Dorado Gold ignores another EC ruling 60/2000EC: 'Maintaining a framework for common action on water policy' which was added onto Greek legislation by the law of 3199/2003. The needs of water for mineral extraction will be equivalent to the needs of 40k citizens and it is predicted that water levels which are +640m above sea level will drop to -140m with a consequent massive destruction of underground water tables. Dust will be produced at the equivalent rate of 4,324 tonnes an hour and the whole region will be equivalent to what occurs in Ptolemaida (the area where electricity is generated through the extraction of lignite which covers 40% of Greece's electricity needs and the EU wants banned!). There will be very large quantities of arsenic, barium, cadmium, chromium, metals, nickel, mercury etc.

E. Tsakalotos Syriza owns shares

Μέχρι που θα φτάνει
η αέρια ρύπανση και η όξινη βροχή
από τα μεταλλεία χρυσού της Χαλκιδικής;

The table shows how far the mineral dust will go and affect a whole region.

Timeline of Police Repression

01.**03.2011 Ierissos'** First big demonstration in which hundreds took part in this town which is closest to the Company's activities.

20.03.2012 Skouries demonstration in the mountain area by 30 citizens. 500 of the company employees attack the locals and the police stood by as people were beaten up.

25.03.2012 Big Tree, Halkidiki had a big demo of all the citizens of the district on a national holiday and a very large force of police confronted them, not allowing them to proceed in a public area. Then with no reason the police attacked the citizens with tear gas and stun grenades. People tried to escape but they were caught short and ambushed by another group of riot police who had planned their entrapment when they retreated.

14.04.2012 Skouries Halkidiki. On 14th April six women went in two cars to the public area of the Kakavos mountain range but in the Skouries point there was a blockade with men from a private security company who were wearing masks. They asked the women for their ID but they refused. After writing down their number plates, they were allowed to continue past the roadblock. But then two farming trucks from Greek Gold threatened them, abusing them and stating they will be blamed for any future problems with Greek Gold Corp, 20 women were held hostage for and the private security company called the police.

05.08.2012 Skouries Halkidiki. Another peaceful demonstration towards the Skouries region and strong police forces refused permission to march despite its having a written confirmation by a public prosecutor. During the negotiations the police forces started to tear gas the people, threw stun grenades and even used plastic bullets. The constant use of tear gas provoked fires in the forest and the fire brigade had to turn up to put them out. In the evening the citizens of Ierissos symbolically blocked the road and they warned the oncoming drivers by distributing information leaflets. After a while they were attacked again.

Citizens and tourists under the guise of damage allegedly made to the local town hall were tear gassed and people were shot at directly rather than rounds being fired in the air. The occupation forces left at midnight.

09.09.2012 Skouries Halkidiki Another peaceful demonstration against the expansion of the company and this time there was a helicopter above the offices of Greek Gold Ltd. along with a very big police presence. With the arrival of the first protestors they were attacked directly with teargas volleys, stun grenades and plastic bullets. People retreated and they were chased by the police. Many demonstrators were injured including the MP Vangelis Diamantopoulos of SYRIZA and a German demonstrator. The biggest injury was the trauma a demonstrator received to his spleen from being hit directly by a tear gas volley.

Riot police militarise the conflict with tear gas and plastic bullets

In October 2012 the police officers union lodged a complaint that illegal procedures were occurring through the use by the police for the private interests of gold mining in Halkidiki without any crime having occurred and without them following correct procedure i.e. article 22 of Law 3938/2011.

21.10.2012 Skouries Halkidiki. More than 2,500 people met at the 'Big Tree' to demonstrate against gold mining in their area. Around 300 remained in this spot whilst the rest marched in the wood towards Skouries. After 7km of walking the police blocked further movement. Fire occurred in the forest and the police and demonstrators together went to put it out. Whilst there, there was a standoff and the head of the strong police force said that they wouldn't use tear gas as happened to the first demonstrators. The demonstrators, women, pensioners etc. retreated once more, and many fell on top of each other and were trodden on; those who remained too close to police lines were beaten up by the police.

Many relatives brought cars to the area to remove the demonstrators and those injured. But the police chased everyone for around 7km. The police attacked some of the convoys as well as breaking car windows, throwing tear gas inside cars, beating up injured protestors. During the attacks the riot police cheered on the attackers and there are eye-witnesses who allege their superiors tried to contain the attacks, for any death would have immense consequences for all involved.

Many were arrested for ridiculous charges, one man for losing control of his vehicle after they had fired a tear gas volley in it. They were refused legal representation and charged with 'attacking the riot police'.

Demonstration in Thessaloniki against El Dorado Gold Corp

25.10.2012 Poligoros Halkidiki. More than 2000 citizens converged on the Ministry of Justice and had a demo in support of the arrested

18.11.2012 Megali Panagia Halkidiki. Demonstration inside the village then a march towards the Kakavos mountain range.

24.11.2012 Thessaloniki Massive demo with more than 8000 people against the destructive mineral extraction in Halkidiki, Kilkis, Thrace. Petitions were handed to the Mayor of Thessaloniki and the Canadian Consul in the city.

Stop the Crime! Stop the Collusion! section of the Thessaloniki demonstration

Outside the Greek Parliament

12.01.13 Athens. 500 citizens travel down from Halkidiki for a demonstration in Athens outside Parliament and the Canadian Embassy.

24.02.2013 Megali Panagia Halkidi. Thousands of citizens from all of Greece demonstrate against the gold mining company once more.

Above is a summary of 26 page bulletin set up by the committee of resistance to El Dorado Gold

http://soshalkidiki.files.wordpress.com/2013/02/soshalkidiki_01_el_sp.pdf

Website in English of Committee

http://soshalkidiki.wordpress.com/category/in-english/

March 2013

'Direct Action' against Multinational Corporate Looting and Destruction of Greece & the Role of Syriza

What happened next is that the offices of the Gold mining company in Skourries were attacked and burnt down. The goverment said 50 masked men did it and that they had broken the cameras. Then they circulated videos of the attack from the same broken down cameras showing a few masked men. **This cannot be explained other than it being a provocation by themselves to blame the surrounding opposition.**

Experience of Keratea: Lessons Learned or Errors to be Repeated?

When Papandreou was in charge with Pangalos (the beached whale) as Vice President, they used alleged EU rules to impose a dump site next to an established community without even having the decency to ask them. The conflict continued unabated with police brutality. But the citizens, without political party domination, continued on their own. They had nowhere to go. This was their houses, their community and they defended themselves up to initiating direct action (modern urban guerrilla warfare). They got night diggers and without the police realising they dug up a main road cutting it in half overnight which meant their area would be cut off from police reinforcements.

They ceaselessly confronted the riot police, tying them down to breaking point. It was heard that their superiors complained to the government that this is the job for an army, not the riot police! Pangalos admitted after the fall of Papandreou that, due to popular protests, the IMF programme could not work after the defeat in Keratea.

House to House Searches and Arrests

Under the pretext of the attacks they started to storm the village of Ierissos arresting most men and doing DNA tests along with body and house searches. They terrorised the population, acting like an occupation army (like Hitler's or the Ottomans) that Greeks have become familiar with in their previous history.

Privatisation and the looting of the natural resources of the country for the sake of large multinational corporations is occurring at the same time as a distinct process of militarisation against all peaceful resistance.

Role of the Left-Syriza

Apart from individual participation, the organised forces of the Left are once more unable to provide a correct focus to the issue which in fact emphasises how in practice the looting of Greece is proceeding apace. Government Ministers sign over national land for its mineral wealth to large multinational corporations and they obviously have a wide range of 'commissioning' activities in their contract bidding (offshore bank accounts made familiar from the Siemens bribery contracts, then require the local police forces to do the 'policing' (enforcing the contracts Cochabamba - Bolivian style) and now they are heading into a Nigerian-Columbia (BP buys army protection) situation where, in order to police the areas surrounding the goldmining sites, there is talk of using foreign mercenaries (ex-Blackwater) or possible use of the army.

SYRIZA is on the pathway to continue where Dimar (Kouvelis-Dem Left) left off is even advertising the GoldMining company in its paper, in the picture below.

Avgi-Syrizas paper advertising Hellas Gold-Skouries

The advertisement says **'One of the Biggest Investments which Greece has Known' 'With Society Next to Us'**!!!

Whatever happens next, one thing is sure: the locals have a chance of winning as they did in Keratea. They have nowhere to go and they can block the exits and entrances to the Gold mining facilities. The mass mobilisations and the unprovoked police attacks which reached the level of tear gassing local schools, arresting little girls to enrage their parents, will provoke even more fury. Out of these popular struggles a new order will be built, one that takes into account the wishes and desires of those who live and toil the land.

VN Gelis

March 2013

April 2013

Stournaras Greek Finance Minister supported 4th Reich against Cyprus-Fake Left plays its Part

Under AKEL which presided over Cyprus joining the EURO (2008) the common view from the non-Greek Left is that the left parties in Greece and Cyprus are bastions of militancy, very few ever really report on their **ACTUAL PRACTICE**. The role of AKEL the sister party of the Greek KKE is ignored for political reasons to show that the 'Left' when in power, isn't involved in implementing IMF imposed austerity programmes (since the era of Milosevic...)

Christofias AKELs leader agreed to the Troika coming into Cyprus after running the country for 5 years and now the German dominated ECB wants to control and centralise all banks in the EU (deciding who gets what loans and for what) so it can dictate monetary policy accordingly, thus ending the independence of ALL nation states, so they embarked on a neo-fascist measures of robbing peoples money under the guise of 'money laundering' whereas no such reasons apply for Luxembourg, Isle of MAN etc or when Daxia asked for E100b and got it. After all it was a French bank so it has importance. Greek ones can go to the wall.

American interests are about selling oil and gas to Europe and minimising the EU's dependence on Russian oil and gas imports. Cyprus has tonnes of deposits, it called in Israeli companies (ie the USA) to extract these resources but none has been sold as they are sitting on it and they have enforced bankruptcy on the island by cutting off the money supply to Cypriot banks. Turkey obviously threatened to blockade Cyprus if it extracted these deposits so they had to rely on a superpower for cover, but now this superpower is out to loot them dry.

Now they have to rely to see what they can get from the Russians if the Americans allow them that is as the last time the Cypriots went against the Americans in the Kofi Annan bi-zone neo-colonial occupation plan, they ended up having many problems, from planes dropping mysteriously out of the sky to allegations that the ex-Premier Papadopoulos was poisoned and his body being stolen from a grave.

This is a re-run of Argentina as the trust in banking has collapsed (banks will be closed for the foreseeable future) by the Eurogroup (Greece voted for the measure) and they want the Cyprus banking system annihilated. The NO vote is the start of the break up of the EZ as there are no limits to the extent the ECB will go to prop up banksters and hoepfully the beginning of the first Iceland within the EZ, where a population can annul all foreign debts and start again afresh. But to do that one has to restore a national currency, capital controls etc and control your own resources and sell them if you want to the highest bidder, not be bankrupted by the ECB so they can then buy your resources for peanuts...

Greece's Role

The government of Samaras, a hard nationalist who rejoined the New Democracy party in Greece after his own chauvinist party hit the rocks a few years ago, is toying with unilaterally declaring an Exclusive Economic Zone in the Aegean – in flat opposition to Turkey.

Kevin Ovenden

Such a 'hard nationalist' is Samaras that when he fought the last election on the platform of the Euro or the Drachma he supported the …Euro.

Since when does Turkey have rights to the Aegean?
He just voted with the Eurogroup to destroy Cyprus, another sign of 'hard nationalism' in that glorious tradition of the Greek ruling class, which allways sided with foreign powers in its history…
He is now trying to flog off Greek importing natural gas companies to the Americans at half the price that they will go to the Russians, another sign of 'hard nationalism'…
Samaras, PASOK and the ex-members of Syriza in the Dem Left are just EU quislings pure and simple.

British bases…
But there is a British base on Cyprus and taking into account Britains colonial past on the island and its role against Makarios, to believe America will give up the island without a fight, I find it hard to believe. Anastasiadis the current President voted for the Anan plan so did Christofias in Akel (not Akel as a whole) and he is still looking to get the money for the Eurogroup by looting Cypriots national pension pots, restructuring the Russian loans outstanding and possibly selling off gas fields whilst attempting to remain in the EZ. Having de facto imposed a haircut on Russian money they have destroyed the banking sector overnight (knock on effects will be mass unemployment, property collapses, political instability etc). The EZ was a disaster waiting to happen now its just a total farce with a beggar thy neighbour 'economic' policy which aims to serve the unelected banksters and their big industrialist friends in the centre and the rest can go to the wall…

Nature of Greece and Cyprus vis a vis Imperialism
As long as imperialism exists and Greece is a neo-colonial muppet
Cyprus will always be at the behest of world powers who will do
what they want when they want to due to its geostrategic location
(spying base for the Arab world). Putin called for the ending of the
dollar as a reserve currency at the G20 again and we are in the midst
of a currency war and Cyprus is a small pawn in the middle.

 The only positive is its part of the EZ chain and even if a small link
is broken in that chain, the link could break.

Update 24. 03. 13
IMF is playing hardball on media reports now asking for a 60% cut
in bank deposits over E100k.
Eurogroup meeting been postponed once more this Sunday and will
allegedly meet tomorrow now ensuring the whole process runs to the
wire or they are waiting to see how it plays out on the stock markets?

They said all Cypriot banks in Greece would be bought for a song by
the Bank of Piraeus but this aint occurred as yet and the workers of
Laiki Bank in Cyprus said they would go on strike on Tuesday.
Other reports have stated that Putin will confront Berlin if Russian
money is touched in Cyprus and strangely enough the oligarch from
the Yelstin era Berezovsky who was given asylum by the UK was
found dead in his bath.

What is also reported is that Russia would have bailed out Cyprus in
totality if it gave them a naval base (as they might lose their only
Mediterrenean one in Syria soon) but the Greek Cypriot Finance
Minister refused to even discuss this. The Archibishop of Cyprus has
called for Cyprus to go bankrupt officially.

Banks have reduced ATM withdrawals now to E100 a day and one
cannot see the banks opening on Tuesday without a default/controls
being imposed in what one can do with ones accounts in the banks,
so this is a trial run to wheel it out across the EZ...as too many
banks exist and there is surplus capital that has to be destroyed just
like products which cant be sold have to be buried.

ΔΕΝ ΞΕΧΝΑΜΕ, ΤΑ ΖΗΤΑΜΕ, ΤΑ ΧΡΩΣΤΑΝΕ!!!
We Don't Forget, We Demand, they Owe it

Agreement Reached - 25th March Greece Independence Day

Two banks are going to shut down, bank deposits over E100k are to be hit (how much and for whom not really clarified), difficult to see how the banks will open as they used to before if capital controls are introduced and some depositors get hit whilst others don't. Its the beginning of DIY banking, in other words they will make it up as they go alone deciding who to steal from and when with no recourse to any rules or laws as they have destroyed their banking system. AKEL complained after calling in the Troika and Anastasiades who is the current premier voted for the Anan plan, so the agenda is to keep the Russians out, gas to go to the Americans and Cypriots to be bankrupted so they can leave the island to big power interests. The NO vote was just a move to present the scenario as a fait accompli in order to force it onto the Cypriot people.

Update 26.03.13

Banks will remain closed until Thursday again so if they dont open then, it will be around two weeks closed, the longest in post war history anywhere on the planet. Cypriots are supposed to be paid by the end of the week (for those working) and the Cypriot banks in Greece havent as yet been handed over to some Greek capitalist crook and there are allegations via Reuters that money has left Cyprus at double the rate over the last month via outlets of Cypriot banks abroad (around Euro 6billion)

The head of the Cypriot Parliamentary group Papadopoulos stated that the options of a return to the CYpriot pound still remain on the table and the govt has stated the haircut will be still around 40% of all deposits over E100k (which also includes pension funds, govt instutions like hospitals, schools etc).

So banksters may drag this out until people protest outside the banks and demand their money Argentinian style, until then the bank heist will proceed accordingly and the instability will affect tourism and business in general as we live in a just in time economy and reducing withdrawals to E100 daily affects every facet of modern life.

The Eurogroup chief who yesteraday stated that this is a blueprint for the 'PIIGS' and then re-called it (after the Euro started to slide) is what their real intentions are. The Cypriot economist Pissarides stated unemployment will reach 30% by the end of the year...

Update 2nd April
To 'save' Cyprus in the way proposed by the troika is to maintain the current system. Yes, if we follow their tactics, we will eventually recover. But at what social and political cost? Capitalism has its booms and busts. After each boom there is a bust and vice versa

George Venizelos
http://leftunity.org/cyprus-faces-organised-robbery-as-eu-leaders-seek-economic-and-political-control/

The current mythology is that capitalism and its crises are like a wheel. They just go round and round and if we wait long enough a 'boom' is coming without a major war or a meltdown of society. If only life were that simple or that capitalism was eternal, then surely a resurrection of the old British Empire must be on the cards.

The other mythology regarding Cyprus is that this is about 'taxing' Russian money not about propping up Deutschebank in a beggar thy neighbour economic policy from the Franco-German controlled ECB.

Capitalism is bust and its banking institutions have fold, they choose which ones of course and under what reasons. Cyprus was chosen for Greece on its Independence Day (25th March) to show that it cannot go against the Troika, it cannot stand on its own two feet and it cannot negotiate with non-EU countries. Having collapsed the Cypriot banking system they aim to collapse Cyprus itself, looting its gas reserves for a pittance with a scorched earth economic policy ALL the politicians in the Cypriot parliament have given cover to.

How the people of Cyprus and Greece react to this latest Troika assault will be key in the coming months…

Update 3rd April 2013
Details of the Cypriot Memorandum has arrived in the media.
GDP is allegedly to fall by 8% though it may be higher if there were more than 100,000 Cypriots employed in financial services of one sort or another.
E70 million in new property taxes
Business tax up from 10% to 12.5%
Wage cuts 4.5% for those up to E1k
6.5% wage reductions for wages up to E1.5k
8.5% wage reductions for wages up to E2k
Reducing the public sector
Privatisations to bring in E1.4b from 2013-16
VAT from 17% to 19%
Add losses from bank deposits for govt institutions such as hospitals and educational institutions and the hit is even higher.

Finance Minister Sarris after signing the handover of Cyprus to the banksters resigned yesterday to be pensioned off with some offshore bonus no doubt, whilst the Cypriot nation will have to scavenge in dustbins to make ends meet…
VN Gelis

Cyprus: lessons from AKEL's shame

Submitted on 22 February, 2013 – 11:22
Author:Theodora Polenta

The Cyprus elections come amidst panic about the collapse of banks and the entire economy of Cyprus – and in the midst of a long strike by construction workers.
In these presidential elections the economy took precedence over the national questions.

A big lead was secured by candidate of the (DHSY), Nicos Anastasiadis, who was also supported by the majority of the Democratic Party (DHKO). He will almost certainly win the second round [post-script: he did win the second round].

The current president of Cyprus, Demetris Christofias of AKEL (the Communist Party), who is going to go down in history as the "communist president" who brought Cyprus under an EU/ ECB/ IMF cuts memorandum, did not seek re-election.

Other candidates were Stavros Malas, supported by AKEL, Giorgos Lilikas supported by EDEK, and the ELAM's Giorgos Charalambous.

ELAM/National Popular Front is a nationalist movement founded in 2008. It describes its ideology as "popular and social nationalism" and promotes Greek nationalism. ELAM's activities include marches against Turkish Cypriots and attacks against immigrants and leftist progressive students.
It is openly connected with Golden Dawn. Golden Dawn leader Ilias Kasidiaris has described ELAM as the "Golden Dawn of Cyprus". Members and supporters of ELAM celebrated Golden Dawns electoral results in the May and June 2012 Greek parliamentary elections on the streets of Cyprus.
Golden Dawn MP Polibios Zisimopoulos attended ELAM's march against the Turkish occupation of northern Cyprus on 20 July 2012. ELAM's announcement of Georgios Charalambous as its candidate

for the presidency was made in the presence of two members of Golden Dawn, Giannis Lagos and Ilias Kasidiaris.

The slight reduction in ELAM's electoral appeal from 4534 votes (1.08%) in the parliamentary elections of May 2011 to 3899 votes (0.885%) on 17 February.

Makaria-Andri Stylianou, candidate for the "Indignant Citizens" movement of Cyprus, scored 1898 votes (0.43%).

Anastasiadis (DHSY) got 45.46%; Stavros Malas (AKEL), 26.91% – down from 33.29% in the 2008 presidential elections; Giorgos Lilikas (EDEK) 24.93%.

61.35% of the voters turned out; it was 75% in the 2008 presidential election.

Because of AKEL's treacherous pro-memorandum politics and austerity measures, the people of Cyprus (those have voted) chose to go with an ardent neo-liberal, a fanatical enthusiast for the EU/ ECB/ IMF Troika, and a supporter of a more severe memorandum. Anastadiasis's electoral manifesto promised that the meagre improvements in workers' living standards and conditions gained during AKEL's presidency would be reversed.

He promised to an end to "laziness" in the public sector, and blamed AKEL's hesitancy and reluctance about the memorandum for the current economic crisis.

His presidency will open the way for the creditors to impose in Cyprus even more destructive cuts than in Greece. But all the presidential candidates, with one or another variant, supported the memorandum framework.

These election results in Cyprus will have very painful side-effects in Greece, whose developments have been heavily influenced by Cyprus throughout the last century.

It is a fact that a sizeable majority of the people in Cyprus are in favour of Cyprus going under a memorandum. Despite being fully aware of the plight of the Greeks and of what they should expect from the memorandum in Cyprus Memorandum, the majority of the Cyprus electorate backed the memorandum.

Christofias and the AKEL leadership have discredited the Left and socialist ideas, and paralysed the left in Cyprus, which normally counts over one third of the voters.

If AKEL had resisted the Memorandum, at least 50% of Cypriots and soon the majority of the Cypriot people would have resisted too.

The coming economic catastrophe of Cyprus is expected to have national implications. "Now or never" was the slogan of the New York Times. The loans that the EU would give to Cyprus's Government "ought to give Brussels leverage to push the Greek Cypriots into cooperating with the Turkish Cypriots in the north of the island to join in a loose federation of the kind proposed in 2004 by Kofi Annan, then the U.N. secretary general ... if European countries want to wield some influence, it is now or never" (4 February).

At this stage, the US and Germany have as their first goal future revenues from undersea deposits of Cyprus gas, and the immediate dismantling of the oversized Cypriot banking system, which is the base of the artificial economic prosperity in Cyprus. The Cypriot banks, according to a recent announcement by the Central Bank of Cyprus, have deposits of over 70 billion euros.

22 billion appear officially as coming from non-European depositors, mainly from Russia and Ukraine. Of the remaining 50 billion, several billion belonging to Russians who in recent years have acquired citizenship of Cyprus.

On 11 February, the Financial Times published the thoughts circulating within the eurozone on the Cyprus banking system. The "radical" scenario includes losses for depositors in the banks and for those who have invested in Cyprus bonds. The financial sector of Cyprus, which today is eight times GDP, would be reduced by one third by 2015.

A more "moderate" option would leave banks half their current size within ten years.

These plans mean sudden recession and economic contraction, disappearance of entire sectors of the economy and massive unemployment (15%, which is a-typical for Cyprus).

Based on estimates of the Troika, Cyprus needs over the next three years around 10 billion euros for recapitalisation of banks and about five billion for fiscal needs.

The memorandum is expected to be completed after March if two conditions are met:

•First, that the loan will be paid in Cyprus will be sustainable. The IMF does not want involvement in the Cyprus Memorandum if the level of public debt after it exceeds 120% of GDP. Future revenues from natural gas do not enter in the calculations, since, as Commerce Minister Neoclis Sylikiotis states, "the first money from the exploitation of natural gas will flow in 2019."

•SECOND, THAT THE DEMAND FROM THE EUROPEAN CENTRAL BANK AND SOME NORTHERN EUROPEAN COUNTRIES TO INVESTIGATE ALLEGATIONS OF LAUNDERING MAINLY RUSSIAN MONEY THROUGH CYPRIOT BANKS, IS MET. THE ISSUE, ACCORDING TO ANALYSTS IN CYPRIOTS, ALTHOUGH REAL, IS RAISED IN A SELECTIVE MANNER, IF ONE CONSIDERS THE PRACTICES IN THE CITY OF LONDON, LUXEMBURG, LIECHTENSTEIN, AND EVEN IN GERMANY ITSELF.

AFTER SIGNING THE MEMORANDUM CHRISTOFIAS DECLARED: "UNITED WE WILL SUCCEED THROUGH HARD WORK AND SACRIFICE IN GETTING CYPRUS OUT OF THIS SITUATION AS OUR NATION DID IN 1974." BUT ULTIMATELY NO SACRIFICES WERE ASKED FROM THE BANKERS, THOSE WHO CAUSED THE CRISIS AND WERE BAILED OUT.

THE ONLY PEOPLE ASKED TO SACRIFICE WERE THE
WORKERS.
CHRISTOFIAS ATTEMPTED TO PRESENT THE
MEMORANDUM AS A VICTORY. BUT IN FACT
CHRISTOFIAS AND AKEL MORTGAGED THE FUTURE OF
THE PEOPLE TO THE BANKS AND THE TROIKA. ALL
CHRISTOFIAS'S SUPPOSEDLY RED LINES WERE DROPPED.

The points of agreement between Christofias and the Troika
included:
•cuts in benefits and social and welfare services
•increasing the retirement age from 63 to 65 years (maintaining it at
63 was an election commitment of Christofias in 2008)
•increase of VAT and indirect taxation
•redundancy for at least 5000 public sector workers.

This is the list of the supposed successes of Christofias's negotiating
skills.
Christofias said he would not give the future revenues from natural
gas to the banks, but he admitted that he would give them a big
percentage. So even the revenues to come after 2019 will be
primarily used to meet the creditors needs.

He said he avoided privatisations! But only as long as "the debt is
sustainable." But the Troika policies, enforcing bank recapitalisation,
will increase the public debt figures hugely.

Christofias also claimed he had preserved ATA (automatic annual
indexation) and the 13th month of pay. But ATA will be frozen for
three years and restored only if there is growth – and then only by
50%. According to calculations by trade unions, under the
memorandum budget workers will lose an equivalent of two months'
wages per year.

 Since Christofias and the AKEL government signed up for a
memorandum last December, a Pandora's box has been opened for a
dismantling of workers' living standards and conditions has been
opened.

For the presidential election, AKEL nominated Malas, who is a technocrat and not a left-winger. That is the culmination of many political compromises and deliberate retreats.

The Christofias government chose a policy of national consensus and unanimity, a policy of management of the capitalist system, a policy of avoiding conflict and confrontations with the bourgeoisie.

The "achievements" of the AKEL government include: acceptance of the memorandum, recapitalising banks without nationalisation, tax immunity of the capitalists and the church.
Now the Left has a duty to focus on the preparation of the only effective weapon available to workers, everyday solidarity and organisation of struggles.

These industrial struggles that are erupting and will erupt are in need of a political leadership. The formation of ERAS is an attempt in that direction.

ERAS did not offer critical support to Malas and AKEL. That stand was based upon the correct assessment that a vote for AKEL cannot be considered a vote for Left policies as AKEL did not put forward even a minimal political manifesto to enable working-class confrontation against the memorandum politics.

ERAS, however, said that it understood that a lot of AKEL voters are still left wing people who voted for AKEL based on their left reflexes.

According to ERAS the main duties of the Left is to dare to do what experience has shown that no Party that intends to operate within the framework of the capitalist system and manage the crisis can achieve – to prioritise ithe reconnection of the combative industrial working-class movement, being fully aware that even the smallest victory requires the utmost determination, rallying and militancy.

For ERAS the main priority is to contribute towards the victory of workers' struggles that have already erupted and prepare; to lay the seeds for the future struggle to come; to strengthen the ideas and the appeal of the left in a radical direction; to form a united front with all workers, Cypriots and immigrants, the rank and file of AKEL and every fighter and campaigner.

The economic crisis has intensified a pan-European offensive of capitalism against the European working class in all countries of Europe. At the same time, massive movements of class solidarity and resistance are developing especially in the countries of southern Europe where economic conditions are worse.

Amongst them are the Cypriot construction workers who have begun to discover from first-hand experience the impact of the memorandum measures.

On Friday, February 8, the general meetings of the construction workers decided to continue their strike, which had already completed 16 days. The management has not accepted any of the compromise proposals of the ministry. The two union federations (PEO and SEK) are under pressure to call a general strike.

The Cypriot construction workers' struggle is certainly not something new. Since 2010 their bosses have refused to sign a new Collective Labour Bargaining Agreement.
After fruitless negotiations and 24-hour and 48-hour strikes, it became apparent to the construction workers that more decisive action was necessary.

Cypriot construction companies have found in the crisis a perfect excuse to dismantle labour rights.
Despite the fact that the construction sector today employs the same number of workers as in 2008, Cypriot bosses have chosen to sack Cyprus construction workers (6,000 redundancies according to the Cypriot trade unions) and to hire workers coming from other countries of the EU (10,000) with lower wages and no coverage by the collective bargaining agreements.

The reaction of the bosses to the strike of the construction workers has been swift and harsh, recruiting scabs.

The AKEL government of AKEL, which claimed to speak in the name of the workers, the Left and socialism, not only did nothing to safeguard the rights of workers and enforce collective agreements for all, but on 5 February sent the police to attack the strikers, arresting three of them! The largest union in Cyprus, especially among construction workers is the PEO, which is controlled by AKEL.

The struggle of the construction workers is a struggle for all workers in Cyprus. The construction workers' struggle should not be seen solely as a fight by one group to maintain their collective bargaining agreements. The workers are fighting for the extension of collective bargaining agreements to every work place and to every worker independent of nationality. Cypriot and foreign construction workers are striking together, giving a strong message of struggle and solidarity.

Over the last few months, Christofias has reiterated over and over again that "he had been forced to sign the memorandum" , "there was no alternative" etc! The truth is that the memorandum is the only solution if one wishes to safeguard the interests of the bankers.

The duty of the Left is not to save the bankers and the capitalists but to prioritise and unequivocally protect the workers' rights. The Memorandum is the end result of the policy of AKEL and Christofias since they came to power.

It's exactly what Cristofias meant when he affirmed the ruling class at home and abroad – in 2008 after the election – that his intention was to manage the system and not to change it. Especially at this time of crisis, however, any effort of a government of the Left to govern via class collaboration and consensus results to a memorandum with "No Human Face" and makes the Left responsible for the crisis in the minds of the working class.

AKEL's years of government were based upon disabling instead of strengthening the trade union movement. One of Christofias's final acts was to invite in the trade union leaders and ask for their collaboration, i.e. no industrial action of any form, in order to smoothly implement the memorandum.

A left government that "does not understand" or "does not want to understand" that the crisis is in the logic of the capitalist system is driven to implement anti working class policies spreading the ideology of defeat and impotence to the working class movement and opening the doors for the original right wing governments to escalate the attacks. At the same time it creates the conditions for the strengthening of the extreme right.

There is an alternative and that is shown daily by the pan European working class movements of resistance against the memoranda and austerity measures and cutbacks of the Greek, Spain, Portuguese, Irish, Italian workers and the re -emergence of the combative working-class movement in the capitalist metropolises of UK, Belgium, France and Germany.

If AKEL were a consistent Left Party, then it should have embraced the following plan of action:
point black refuse for the workers to take the burden of the debts of the bankers and suffer the "support mechanisms" of the EU and Troika.

-to nationalise the collapsed banks under workers' and social control
-measures to fight tax evasion and fraud, taxing wealth, capital, banks and church
-stop repayment of installments and interest on the debt, as the debt repayments are beyond the limits of Cyprus workers and society.

To the extent that the dilemma is posed, "Payment of the debt versus payment of salaries and pensions", a Left's government answer must be: "In order to pay salaries, refuse to pay the debt"
nationalisation of banks, nationalisation of industries in crisis (construction, tourism, etc.) and commerce under a planned economy, under conditions of workers' and social control and management for the needs of society and not for the profit of the bankers and the rich.
There are lessons for Syriza in Greece.

The results of the elections of 17 June and the spectacular rise of Syriza have stirred up debate on the relationship between parliament and the Left, the Left and the state, and the Left the movements and, especially, the tactics and strategy of the Left.

The route of AKEL has a lot to teach us. The strategy of AKEL, that is the policy of the reformist Left, roughly consisted of the following: the goal of any struggle in the political and trade union sphere was the entrance of the left in government. The goal of socialist revolution and workers' power was abandoned as a target "for the moment" and replaced with the entry into government. For the purpose of entering the government and making bargains with the bourgeoisie, control and blocking of the mass movement becomes essential.

The period when Christofias signed the memorandum was not a period of defeat of the working class movement. All around Europe and especially on the South Europe and Greece we witnessed international class solidarity and the re emergence of a combative working class movement that refuses to surrender to the memorandum politics and austerity measurements.

If AKEL and Christofias had refused to enter the memorandum and adopted a program of transitional demands to remobilise the trade union movement (where AKEL has the majority), then it would have triggered a wave of class solidarity and support both from the Cyprus working class, from the Greek workers, from the South European workers, and from all the workers in Europe, who would have seen AKEL's government as part of their political struggle for a government of the Left to scrap all memoranda and all anti working class laws.

However, AKEL choose the path of compromise and "social peace." AKEL asked the working class to accept and bear the "brunt of the sacrifices imposed by the struggle against the crisis" with the following reasoning: first Capitalist growth, competitiveness and exist from the bankers crisis and after that, pro-working-class reforms in the state and economy. AKEL took responsibility for rescuing the Cypriot capitalism from its own crisis.

Syriza should be clearly separated from such paths of "responsibility" and "governability" and class collaborationist legalistic politics.

The people who voted for Syriza and the rank and file of Syriza endured an unprecedented campaign of ideological bullying (from inside and outside Greece), and do not expect from Syriza a "responsible" opposition. They want Syriza to offer an alternative narrative – that there is life outside the Memoranda, and to organize the resistance to overthrow the memoranda and austerity measures. For a government of the left dialectically linked to the workers' struggles, as a first step to social change, where people will not only be "before profit", but will determine their own lives …

Syriza has a duty to contribute towards the strengthening of the pan European working class alliance from below against the bosses' European Alliance of austerity and memoranda. This alliance will be built: between the Iberian protesters and the Italian strikers, between the Greek labor movement and the French Peugeot workers, between the Cypriot construction workers and the UK anti cuts movement.

All European Left forces should take the lead in the working class pan European coordination of struggles: with joint demonstrations and organization of international solidarity and support to major labor struggles that will bring closer the goal of a large pan-European general strike.

This criterion determines the programs of the Left which should only speak with the rank and file working class movement: The overthrow of austerity, abolition of the debt, zand war against the national bond holders and creditors would relieve the nightmare experienced by both "North" and "South" workers. "No sacrifice for the euro" will unite all labour movements against the blackmailers of Brussels.

In such an orientation, the left can be a leader, to play the historic role that corresponds to the current conditions of capitalism under deep crisis. The commitment to develop a pan-European resistance movement, the head-on collision with the EU's ultra-neoliberal policy, can create the conditions for a response to the crisis and counterposed to the bosses' European Union the workers' red Europe.

All we have left is a pair of underpants which have been mended, tell us when you need them and we will have them SOILED! (Anti-auterity protestors)

June 2013

6. Eyewitness Reports ERT Occupation

Closure of ERT-Greece's Main State Broadcaster

Burning the EU Flag at the ERT Occupation

Was at the Occupation of the state broadcaster last night till 3 am.
Thousands of people kept on coming. At the headquarters of ERT in
Agia Paraskevi where present both the KKE and Syriza and assorted
leftists on top of thousands of people who had come to show
solidarity to the mass sacking of 3,000 people.

Questions were asked to Stratoulis Syriza MP why dont they leave
the Troika occupied Parliament and stop waffling endlessly and call
the people to struggle to get rid of the Troika, he said we are looking
into that. One of his parliamentary minions stated we are with the
People and we keep on getting teargassed, as if they are the only
ones. Tsipras could have asked for an emergency debate in
Parliament as Leader of the Opposition and taking into account that
neither PASOK or DIMAR even knew this was coming so fast, but
did not. GD announced indirectly that they are happy with the
sackings as they aint allowed on state TV.

I judged that there must have been more than 50k people that turned up last night. They said the riot police was going to break through but it didn't. They shut down all digital signals so all foreign media outlets, BBC, CNN, Euronews are closed as well. The KKE is rebroadcasting from its own station in analogue signal the occupied ERT colleagues broadcasts. Last time the Greek state media was shut down was during the last German occupation in 1940.

Greek TUC-ADEDY is meeting to allegedly see if it will call a General Strike. Another solidarity demo is called for today at 5pm.

VN Gelis

ERT: Appeal to foreign media and journalists

In News on June 12, 2013 at 10:27 am

pic by @polyfimos

Yesterday the Greek government (primarily New Democracy party, without the support of coalition partners PASOK and DIMAR) announced they would shut down ERT, Greece's national broadcaster. The argument was that ERT is marred with corruption and that it operates at a cost to the public sector. First, ERT is profitable, as its employees testify. Second, the New Democracy spokesman Kedikoglou who announced the decision and raged about "corruption" was the same politicians that has requested the hiring of 23 of "his" people in ERT!

More importantly, the decision was not approved by the parliament, but was implemented through a ministerial decree (which is a violation of the Constitution and Greek legislative procedure). The decree is now at the office the President of the Hellenic Republic and parties opposing it have contacted him NOT to sign it. Neo-nazi Golden Dawn and New Democracy are the only 2 parties that have openly supported the decision (although it seems coalition partners were aware of it).

The decision was announced during the day and at 11pm riot police went to Mount Ymittos and turned off the digital and analogue signals. ERT was still broadcasting and used TVE (Spanish), and 902 channels (owned by the Communist Party), among others. A couple of hours later DIGEA (private operator of digital signal in Greece) turned off the 902 channel, claiming it should not broadcast ERT!

ERT employs more than 2500 people and operates channels across Greece, in remote areas where other broadcasters have no signal. It also broadcasts across the world, informing Greeks living abroad and providing a live link to them with Greek culture and "home". Protesters gathered outside the ERT building until 3 am in the morning and they are gathering again today.

Here in London, a demonstration has been organised to support ERT employees, at 5pm London time at the Greek Embassy W11 3TP.

This is the facebook link
http://www.facebook.com/events/551233141581740/551427951562259/?notif_t=plan_mall_activity

This is the announcement by the European Federation of Journalists.

http://europe.ifj.org/en/articles/closure-of-public-broadcaster-in-greece

This is the announcement by the European Broadcasting Union.

http://www3.ebu.ch/cms/en/sites/ebu/contents/news/2013/06/ebu-urges-greek-government-to-re.html

This is a petition to stop the shutdown of Public Television in Greece.

http://www.avaaz.org/en/petition/Stop_the_shutdown_of_Public_Television_in_Greece/?awfVmdb

Please follow #ERT on twitter to find out more.

Please write about this and support us, we have no other outlet except internet and foreign broadcasters.

This is about freedom of speech and right to independent information.

Thank you in advance for your support.

Update 13.06.13

There was a mini-General Strike today one of those that affect primarily the public sector. For the first time in 3.5 years the KKE was at the same location as the sellouts of the Greek TUC (thats how they refer to them) Around 15k in all (but people keep on coming and going so the number could be double) but the KKE matched the others (ADEDY Public Sector Unions-Syriza-assorted leftists).

The KKE seems to be implementing the policy of its minority by turning up in joint with others at the same location and remaining instead of going home immediately after a brisk walk and chanting the same slogans they wheel out constantly (they might go full whack the other way and drop from standing around too much!) It is broadcasting the occupation but the govt keeps on disabling the signal and Stournaras announced today that whoever broadcasts the signal will be in contempt of court. The reason they gave for the immediate closure was that otherwise they would have had endless strikes. But it appears both PASOK and Dimar are talking harakiri and by the end of next week we will know if the govt is going to go to new elections.

Syriza has called for what appears to be a pre-election rally in Sindagma sq Monday night and on Monday the Greek Troika will meet to see if they can continue to rule together. The way ERT has been closed is aiming to be the blueprint for Hospitals, Schools, University and Army units.

If they weaken the nightly occupation of the ERT headquarters the riot police may come in at 5am as they did with the Underground workers but that will occur in joint with the union misleaderships who will give the order to demobilise.

Update 14.06.13

Demos continued all day outside ERT in Athens.

75 cadres of PASOK led by Skandalidis want Venizelos (party Leader) to drop out of the governing coalition. There are severe frictions in the other coalition partners of Dimar (Dem Left ex-Syriza).

Samaras offerred an olive branch today alleging he will rehire a smaller amount of journalists and re-open ERT by the end of next week. In the meantime the head of the European Public Broadcast Union turned up in Athens criticising the govts actions.

ERT was transferred from the Ministry of Culture to the Ministry of Economics deiberately to be shut down and it appears it was a condition of the neo-fascist Eurogroups next bailout tranche of E3.3billion.

One cannot work out at this stage what is being played as the problem will emerge that the building will have to be vacated by the employees for it to reopen with less employees and that cannot occur unless the union leaders do a back door deal and call for them to empty it. The volume of people on the outside make a storming of the building by the riot police impossible as well. The corridors are long and there are many and there are at least 5 floors with two or more underground with expensive equipment, but knowing the gangsters that rule anything is possible.

Update 15/16.06.13

Tsipras Poster calling for Demo in Sindagma on 17th June (one year to the date Samaras won the election)

One can discern the **red background** from the man who will accept NATO and has met the top financial elites from Schauble, Brookings Institute and the LSE..

Large numbers of people were outside ERT most of Saturday and at night the Greek symphony orchestra played a free concert. At a certain stage in the late evening they reported on events in Taksim and gave out solidarity greetings to the fighters there for freedom.

The two parties in the coalition remain still in conflict with Samaras and do not agree with the middle road option of reopening it with fewer staff next week. So we could be going to a third option of Samaras resigning after the disaster with the privatisations that have fallen through (with Russians due to EU-USA involvement) and appointing another muppet until new elections are called for maybe after the German elections.

Today they are having a party which has a title 'Come and Eat as we Didn't Eat Anything' in response to the ex-Vice President of Greece Pangalos (PASOK) who stated that 'We ate it All' hence we needed the Troika.

In Thessalonikis station it has for the first time tried to change its programme (from when it was govt owned and was pure propaganda and globalism) to show a programme regarding Halkidiki gold mine protests, the occupation of an engineering firm etc.

The pension funds of the journalists haven't been merged as yet they are the last to go and this is also on the cards as ERT was the biggest employer.

Update 17/18.06.13

Syrizas Main Rally in Sindagma Square Billed to be one of Overturning the Tripartite Coalition

There were many developments yesterday as there were two rallies

(one by Syriza in the main Athens square and one by the KKE near the ERT tv studios in Agia Paraskevi) as well as a meeting of the three party coalition and a decision of the Supreme Court regarding the closure of ERT.

During Sunday evening late they circulated the first free paper called 'Independent Press' by the strikers from the media (without stating which media and who it belongs to for fear of reprisals) Inside the edition they had an interview with the leader of the Metro Workers Stamatopoulos who stood on the Antarsya electoral ticket and who was involved in the big sellout of the Metro Workers stating we need a new

(http://imfoccupationgreece.blogspot.gr/2013_01_01_archive.html) revolt whilst in practice organising nothing.

At the same time we had the circulation of Rizospastis by the KKE on Sunday and on Monday by Avgi of Syriza thus both breaking the journalists strike. Tremis the leader of the Journalists Union condemnded the KKE as 'strikebreakers' though who has done what is unlear and why as the strike was supposed to go on till Tuesday morning but was broken by all the private media on Sunday as well.

Throughout the whole of Monday the main point of contention was that 'no one wants elections' and this will cripple Greece so the tone for compromise was set, by the Tripartite Coalition. Under the background of the Surpreme Court (which stated that ERT should reopen) the Govt on paper backed down (pending the arrival of the German Finance Minister Schauble today) saving the coalition govt from collapse. What the actual decision means in practice or whether they are bying time for a few days no one can really know.

Syrizas rally in Sindagma billed as a 'rally for the overturn' of the Govt had very few participants taking into account they are the official opposition they couldn't even fill one third of Sindagma sq (PASOK's Andreas Papandreou in his heyday in the early 80's filled 1.5squares). The KKE's rally had a few thousand as well on the other side of Athens.

So far Syriza hasn't put forward a vote of no confidence has refused to leave Parliament and has allowed the situation to be dictated by the Tripartite Coalition when it has become common knowledge that the Greek govt no longer runs in any way on a parliamentary level but on dictat from the overseas Troika, with Acts of Legislative Enforcement which require no parliamentary majority (20 have been carried out so far) and half the working population is under a civil protection notice (ie cannot strike).

A significant occupation which has degenerated into a pop concert nightly with the support of the parties of the fake Left will end up being another missed opportunity to focus and channel the anger of the Greeks into a different direction, one which seeks conflict not compromise with the internal and external Troika...

23rd June 2013-

ERT occupation has continued unabated but the political will to take it a step further organising roving pickets and uniting with other areas of the public sector that are facing shutdown does not seem to be there from any significant wing of the Employees. The govt has offered two months redundancy pay and the departure of Syrizas ex-faction Dem Left from the Greek Tripartite Coalition has dented Samaras auythority to such an extent that he exists only because of the fakeness of the Opposition.

Commentators have noticed that Syriza does not want to govern and being unable to capitalise on this gravest of crises for the govt it did not once more stand the test of crisis. From early on Tsipras stated that the Tripartite coalition would not be brought down by its partners and when Ind Greeks put in a motion of 'no confidence' they refused to back it. The offer of 2,000 re-employment on 3 months contracts from the 2,700 employed at ERT is the carrot to split the labour force and silence any radical voices. Having an organised presence that is what Syriza is doing ensuring the radical nature of the occupation fizzles out over time, the riot police storm the building one evening and the whole thing is hived off to private tv operators (role model once again for the rest of the EU).

The govt's reshuffle of Ministers that have departed from Dem Left and now to be taken over by PASOK shows the absolute merging of

New Democracy and PASOK as well as a few MP's from Dem Left who want to support the new govt reshuffle. In the background to all of this the Chinese company called COSCO is to increase its ownership of Piraeus ports to 51% and the privatisation of the gas import company DESFA which no longer has a Russian bid has been given to an Azeri company at half the original price (now they realise the govt is a busted flush).

The IMF's direct intervention that if Greece goes for elections now they would withdraw the 'funding' ie collapse the economy shows that Greece is no longer run by Greeks in any shape or form, but multinational operators for transnational corporations and their banking system and anything that questions their right to rule must be crushed one way or another...

Update 28.06.13

The 'new' govt which is just a rehash of the old without the official backing of Syrizas ex-cdes in Dem Left has put in certain hyperglobalists in neuralgic ministries. The son of the German collaborator friend of the Bush clan in Greece and ex-PM Mitsotakis, Kiriakos as Minister of the Civil Service to continue its destruction where the previous one left off, Manitakis.

Kedigoglou who left his position in charge of ERT has now become Minister of Education to privatise and shut down nurseries, schools and universities around 15k educationalists have been earmarked for that.

Adonis Georgiadis has been appointed Minister of Health to proceed with the closure of Hospitals (6 so far in the Athens region). He was a leading member of LAOS the grouping which had the positions of Golden Dawn before they joined the banksters Papadimos govt after Papandreous departure and then suffered an electoral wipeout. This party for years was labelled neo-nazi before GD took the mantle.

The labour force at ERT has been given two months redundancy pay and lists are being drawn up as to who will be reassigned to the new company and a letter was circulated to staff to protect the equipment there. Last night one of the Kouris bros who had the main publishing arm of PASOK (Avriani newspaper) and then had tv stations was stating he wants to reopen ALTER tv station to fill the void of collapsed ERT and initial viewing figures show that with no ERT the private tv stations which have been on the brink for a long time are profiting in viewing numbers.

So if half the labour force is forced out and they don't go the govt has only the option of using riot police to intervene (they said they wouldn't) so it becomes an issue for the ERT union POSPERT how they sellout half the labour force.

Yesterday there were three demos in central Athens (Katselis breadmaking firm with 500 sackings) outside the Economics Ministry, hospital workers outside the Ministry of Health and arms workers from EVO-Pirkal. ERT workers could have held demos in the centre, they haven't and called for unity on their pirate station so far this hasn't occurred. To each his own and to each in defeat, seems to be the prevailing view.

An unemployed metalworker in Pireaus district is reported to having his house repossessed for income tax charges of E1,600 in the KKE's daily Rizospastis.

Epilogue

The candidate which Syriza voted for in the position of the Journalists Union ESHEA ended up supporting the new scab tv called NERIT.

6. Syrizas Neo-american path. Setting up a unified pro-EU entity to honour foreign banksters debts.

July 2013

Syriza's First Congress: Maastricht's Children Coming Back with a Vengenance

"With tough negotiations for the debt.

With the aim of erasing large part of the debt, adding a growth clause, and
freezing loan interest repayment.

With a strong Alliance of the South.

With the aim of an international convention for the debt, similar to the London
Agreement on the German debt in 1953.

These positions, which to some might sound utopian, will become material power and will gain much more international support when SYRIZA emerges from the elections as a majority party and the Left forms a new government.

And do you know who with their attitude show they believe in SYRIZA? Those who fear SYRIZA."

Tsipras Speech from Syriza Conference

We have gone from *a unilateral cancellation of the debt, the abolition of the Memoranda* overnight to a.... **European Convention on the debt.**

After one year with ***three serious battles*** (Halkidiki gold mine, Metroworkers strike and public tv ERT closure) the electoral polls for Syriza have constantly been below the 27% they got in the last elections. The 'closer' it gets to power, the more it accommodates to Greece's 'creditors' and this isn't lost on the electorate. Paid professional politicians are precisely that, they will say and do anything at any moment in time of their choosing without even a blink of an eyelid. Tsipras ***isn't a break with the past, but a continuation of it.***

Maastricht's children are finally coming full circle.

October 2013

Security Services Job? Two GD murdered at point blank range...Minister Mitsotakis calls for Martial Law

Two dead Golden Dawn Members

In what appears to be the standard hallmark of a security services job two GD members outside their offices in N Ionia a suburb of Athens were gunned down in what was the tradition of 17N style of execution. Men wearing motorcycle helmets shot at point blank range three GD members according to reports. Two are dead as they emptied their bullets in them. The third allegedly escaped so far.

Kiriakos Mitsotakis - son of the Mitsotakis clan (the premier Bilderburg Quisling political dynasty of Greece) who in his role as Public Sector Minister has presided over a mass job cull of 25k workers in the recent period was interviewed in the Belgian press this week calling for martial law to implement the 'reforms' is the total firesale of Greece.

Since early September when a mass coordinated campaign against Golden Dawn was inaugurated by the global corporate media in alliance with the Quisling administration of the Troika in Greece led by Samaras and Venizelos (ND and PASOK) the Greek corporate media with interests in the Gold Mines of Skouries started selling the theory of the 'two extremes' of the Right and the Left.

The fake Left jumped on this bandwagon playing along having protest after protest over the murder of Fissas helping to derail thus a massive strike wave which was cut short due to his murder. Instead of pointing the case towards the security services as with the murder of the Bank workers at Marfin they sold the theory of the ...'right extremist'.

The journalist-whores who make up the Greek corporate media are willing to sell the theory 'of the two extremes' in order to declare martial law, the plans for which were announced in the Belgian media by Mitsotakis junior (known as the Bush clan of Greece). This is repetition once more of the Gladio style provocation campaigns that rocked Italy in the 70's.

Since September they have adopted the nazi rule of collective liability and have locked up GD MP's banned them from collecting the state subsidy given to all the other political parties and started a massive witchhunt against them.

The state will now start to make links with 'red' terrorists and associate this criminal act to justify its state sponsored terrorism: **mass sackings. mass closures of schools and hospitals. mass suicides etc**. They have blood on their hand and they seem determined to continue along that path. They have no other path. Capitalism is collapsing and it will sink everything in its path unless its overthrown

2nd November 2013
GD MP's in Parliament have stated that a police car was stationed outside the party offices in N Ionia for the last month and absent last night when the killing took place. Alongside Syriza they are calling for calm for peoples reaction to the event.

November 2013

Syriza's No Confidence Vote

After his trip to Texas and Washington (we still don't know who he met there and what was the nature of the discussion) we heard that the only way the Eurozone can be saved is by saving the European south. Tsipras put his no confidence vote once the plane had landed. So did he work this out on the way back from the States or was there a discussion with other members of the leadership by phone from the USA?

Having no hope of winning as no confidence votes have never shown a break in the ruling party formations as ND has a 50 MP bonus he managed to achieve 124 votes with GD, KKE, Ind Greeks voting with his motion with the knowledge of course that only MPs from PASOK and ND could bring down their own government. In the end one PASOK MP voted against and was expelled and another claimed he was ill and didn't turn up to vote. The main area of dispute has been the new taxes on agricultural land and property plus liberalising all repossessions, which has seen around 70 ND MPs baulking at the vote. Stratoulis from Syriza had stated that PASOK previously in 2011 had won a No Confidence vote but soon thereafter Papandreou was given his marching orders. Hence the question remains what does Tsipras know we don't and why did he place the No Confidence Vote?

Only a few thousand turned up at the Sindagma rally showing that Syriza once more has no actual support in society and the vote to it was a reaction to all else than support for its EU neo-liberal policies.

So what is going on. The Troika cannot impose any more new taxes, the ruling parties have fragmented and ND is on the way to becoming the new PASOK. It has been in power for 16 months around the same time Papandreou lasted from when he called the IMF into Greece way back in May 2010. Samaras is now a busted flush his bonapartist measures whereby paramilitary shootouts occur to generalise the theory of the 'two extremes' (murders of antifascist

rapper and two GD members) go nowhere and the crisis continues unabated with around 25k public sector workers to be fired by Xmas and 150-250k earmarked for the following two years.
Unemployment continues to rise and the scenes of young people scavenging in dustbins is widespread in Athens. We have seen scenes of ruling party MPs calling their own ministers Leninists for wanting to take away peoples property! The conclusion is we have a ruling crisis and this flows from the fact that people no longer have any money to pay the endless array of taxes. The state is shutting down and deregulating its operations. The Universities have been closed since they opened after the govt fired a majority of its admin staff. Hospitals aren't functioning and thousands of doctors have been given their marching orders.

In order to forestall an inevitable social explosion they will either cut Samaras short replacing him with another joker of the style of Papadimos or bring Syriza to power. That is where the fun will start for Syriza will try to solve the unsolveable: remain in the Euro whilst cancelling all payments to the debtors.

If there is a pan-European move in that direction due to the fact that the Euro-sceptics have the upper hand in two major countries (France and UK) in the forthcoming Euro-elections and the fact that the role of the German finance ministry hasn't been assigned alongside Brussels starting an investigation into the full impact of Germany surpluses, the Tsipras move is part of a wider plan. If on the other hand Tsipras wanted to bring down the government he could have called for all the MP's who voted with him to withdraw from Parliament as he did mention that the govt rules on Executive Decrees 22 in total in other words an IMF junta with the façade of Parliamentary democracy but he could have, but didn't.

Without a return to national currencies a restoration of border controls in capital goods and labour and a national strategy to restore economic activity as a first step to restore growth that gives people work and a livelihood and the dissolution of the EU and the EZ we will continue to go from bad to worse. This crisis isn't going away.

February 2014

Syrizas Regional Governor Candidate for Messinia-Kalamata Odysseas Voudouris IMF Stooge with neo-nazi links

Syrizas announcement that Odysseas Voudouris is to be the candidate for Regional Governor for the Pelopponese and his statement that 'he does not regret that he voted for the IMF-Memorandum that came to Greece' has created ruptures in the Syriza bankdwagon.

His statement is only the tip of the iceberg if one goes through his autobiography which existed on the Dem Left web site iefimerida

He started his party career when George Papandreou found him due his known appreciation of 'movements'. Papandreou made him in charge of the Citizens movements trying to weaken the influence of the Simitis faction within PASOK during his own rise into PASOK.

Voudouris Voted for the IMF-Memorandum package Papandreou introduced into Greece and supported it vociferously in the mass media. He voted for it and supported and in December 2011 when the Indignants from Kalamata considered him as much as supporter of the Memorandum but also a Quisling greeting him with a banner

'Quisling out of our City' with the known slogans of the time 'Bread Peace Freedom, the Junta didn't Die in 1973'

Greeting Voudouris in Kalamata in 2011 with the banner Quislings Out!

The next day on the central media outlet Alter Voudouris supported the IMF and Papandreou and condemned Syriza for the attacks he received in Kalamata! He also stated that the IMF package was the only solution for reducing the deficit and supported that Greece in one year would have a budget surplus!

Voudouris support to the IMF was so strong that he sent a letter to Papandreou then asking him to throw out of the govt all those Ministers who place obstacles or bring opposition to these measures! 'Pseudo-dillemmas and personal practices which only postpone into the future the necessary decision with a greater cost for all. Whilst a few Ministers fight decisively without taking into account the political cost others don't follow that path. We consider it an imposition that all the members of the govt which can't cope with the pressure of the circumstances or place a priority in their personal path to leave this govt'…

Whilst the clouds were heavy for PASOK and all showed that Papandreou is nearing his end Voudouris voted against the 2nd IMF package. He ended up biting the hand that feeds his stating 'a bankrupt has just expelled me'! Voudouris said that he was expelled from PASOK by a President whilst he management has finished and his politics have failed.

Rushed to Kouvelis Dem Left

No one understood how he jumped ship and ended up in Kouvelis-Dem Left and held a big party in the café Black Papias in the Athens centre greeting him. Voudouris then goes on to state my cooperation with Dem Left "isn't a provisional choice for electoral purposes. It's a political act which is based on my permanent position that it is my wish to ask for a change of course with the participation of the Left, which is being called to accept government positions"

Kouvelis then proposed his to stand as an MP and he became one joining Dem Left campaign in 2012.

se

ΠΑΣΟΚ

The son of political refugees he was born in Budapest and grew up in France. His parents returned provisionally in 1965-67 and they were chased out again and Voudouris then grew up and studied in France. Voudouris Graduated from the Medical School of Paris with specialism in surgery. Was prosecuted for medical negligence as well. In his autobiography he claims that he took part in the insurrection of May 1968 and the French student movement of 1970

He took part in humanitarian movements in war zones.

He became a regional governor of the Greek health service appointed by Simitis and Papandreou also place him in the National Council for Foreign Policy (2003-4)

In an article in the Ta Nea it is stated he ended up in politics as he was thrown out of the 'Doctors Without Borders'

After taking part in Dem Left which was in the Samaras-Venizelos quisling administration he now attacks Kouvelis for -ND in govt.

Mayoral Circus

Syriza is imposing PASOK candidates from above and ND has more than one candidate showing that it is openly split. The crisis of the ruling party is now being openly being transformed into a crisis of the opposition party. In Macedonia Syriza subtracted another candidate as he mentioned Israel and banks in one interview.

The pro-EU parties are on a fast track to disintegration…

Member of the Restis and Pallis Foundation

The Ethnos newspaper (belonging to the Bobolas corporation Hellenic Gold and Road tolls fame) states that he is related to the scandal Karouzou (money laundering) and Restis friend Anastasios Pallis (shipowner with neo nazi infatuations)

The 'museum' of shipowner Pallis

.

Ethnos continues and states that Voudouris is also a member of the pallisfoundation.

These are Syrizas newfound electoral candidates: shipwrecks from PASOK who spend time anywhere just to be elected and continue their pro-IMF agendas!

Appendix

(i)Debate on the closure of ERT with Bob Archer Greek Solidarity Committee

For Bob,

-There was a significant general strike during the 40's under the German occupation in Athens and hundreds of thousands went on demos when Bulgaria annexed Greece during the occupation. Strikes will always occur in Greece occupation or not. The issue at stake is why the parties of the fake left don't leave Parliament and campaign on the streets to overthrow the Troika, that is what the difference is. For the simple reason is that they are embedded to the system, funded by it, promote it at every available opportunity and like yourself believe this is about stabilization theory (whatever that is!) not about a general decline and downfall of the last Capitalist Empire – the USA. It's a difference to be a party of 4% and a party of 27% and when unemployment is one third of the population not to be able to fight for power (unless of course that is precisely what the Euros-Syriza don't want to do). Syriza has spent the last six months going round the world promoting itself as the party that will save the EU and the Euro in all the worlds imperialists centres. A far cry from even the capitalist PASOK in its heyday.

That is why when they had their first national meeting in Sindagma they could fill only a small section of the bottom part of the square (around 20k) with ERT still being fresh in everybody's mind.

As for ERT they are buying time aiding the union sellouts that run the occupation to bore everyone to death with pop concerts and video clips about 9/11 and the 'moon' landings you uploaded, until August. The issue of ERT though is the new format of closures for hospitals, schools, transport (all that belong to the state sector) ie immediately with no warning here and and now.

-The Greek political class were never de-nazified as opposed to the rest of Europe even nominally. Churchill promoted and supported the Greek collaborators inaugurating the Greek civil war against the Left. This was then supported by the British Labour party who had 5k troops stationed there throughout the 40's. The cold war was inaugurated in Greece and with the use of napalm the Americans aided the defeat of the partisans. It is this post war American order that is collapsing in Greece as the parties of the bourgeoisie which use to secure 80-85% of the vote now hover below 20% if that.

So when the fake Left with PASOK and Dem Left march against GD they do it to bolster their own anti-fascist credentials and bolster New Democracy (direct heirs to the quisling administration of Tsolagoglou who run Greece during the 3rd Reich) and when council workers in their thousands march with nazi uniforms aboard a tank with banners saying 'Down with the 4th Reich', you go on to dismiss this or ignore it as if :

a) it never happened

b) what it actually means in practice

You then wheel out the old Healyite fake 'build the leadership' stuff as a red herring. Pray do tell me how Healy built the leadership supporting Arafat, the union sellouts in Cowley (against his own workers base) and receiving money from oil-igarchs to prop up a daily only members ever read?

-You argued there could be no possibility of rights being gained within the confines of a nation state and I asked you how to explain the rights accrued to workers over the last two centuries? There is no solution for the Greek masses if they don't fight for national sovereignty, against the EU and globalization which destroyed the country, it has to make a sharp break if it wants to remain intact, otherwise it might as well be broken apart, hived off and the Greeks go the four corners of the earth. Only the Left can save Greece from destruction and no one else will do it for them, but not the current globalised left which like the transnationals is anti-Greek, promotes America at every available opportunity and has become the new napalm to contain popular anger and expression.

Not all countries are in the same situation. When Britain was privatizing in the 80's and attacking one section of industrial worker after another until they destroyed the labour movement, Greece was nationalizing the main sectors of its industries. Up until 1992 it had a very strong labour movement and they were able to bring down the Mitsotakis govt over attempted privatization of the buses. Now Greece has gone the other way and is the fastest in attacking wages and conditions (40-50%) more than any other EZ country. But parallel to that a whole new reserve army of workers came into Greece (equivalent in number) from the ex-stalinist states and the KKE refused to organize them instead becoming foremen in what proved to be the massive building boom of the last two decades (which collapsed in 2008) and has led to a near total meltdown as building involved around 150 odd subsidiary employment industries. Parallely there is no social welfare when unemployed here unlike in the imperialist centres, so one cannot but see an Argentinian style explosion, default and a return to a national currency.

I didn't put forward many views I just wrote what I saw was happening during the ERT occupation. Dan intervened to argue that Greece was propped up by the EU and development occurred in roads and bridges, then he used data from the EU and a shipowners daily to quote on the development of Greece. I countered with data from a KKE economist. In that dispute you were absent again. It is black and white. Either Greece benefited from the EU or it didn't or to put it another way if it hadn't joined the 'Lions Den' (EDA-precursor to Syriza in 1960) would Greece have avoided bankruptcy and developed (even within the confines of capitalism) or would have arrived at the sorry state it is today? Either capitalism is collapsing or it isn't? Like I said previously in your youth you subscribed to breakdown theory when there was full employment now in you old age when mass unemployment is upon us you argue in similar terms like Dan (that we know from where we are where the system is going and that an upturn is upon us) when it is being propped up artificially by QE. I aint that optimistic for capitalism.

VN Gelis

Bread, Peace, Freedom the Junta Didn't Die in 1973

(ii) Drachma or Euro? Default on Way

For the corrupt mass media a return to the Drachma equals destruction! For what reason they don't say. It is served as an honour and explanations don't exist. It is destruction, because it is ...destruction, pure and simple!

"Catastrophic for Greece was how it was characterised by a journalist Ev Mitilinaios the scenario of returning to the drachma" we read in the VIMA newspaper, without anywhere the argument being justified.

The same goes for Papariga (leader of the KKE) who actually doesn't tire in warning us: "A return to the drachma under the current conditions would be catastrophic"!
The why and how must be held only for themselves.

Also the European specialists speak about destruction but we understand them e.g. The president of the European central bank, Z. C. Trichet who supports that it will be: destructive for the Eurozone the return to the drachma. He doesn't say this for Greece. We would agree with him, with the meaning that a departure of Greece from the Eurozone would mean the end of an opportunist, stupid and criminal attempt to impose a united currency without a united economy and state. The responsibility belongs to the architects of the EU and the Eurozone, with the victim being Greece and the other countries of the European South.

There are others who state that due to the lack of a similar experience, the honest reply to the question as to 'what will happen if we return to the drachma' is simply, 'I don't know'!

We Have Experience

In reality there is experience not from one but many countries. Typically they aren't the same, but essentially they don't differ. Before we analyse things more, let us give a hypothetical preliminary example so one can be better understood:
Let us assume we had held onto the drachma but had latched it onto a hard currency, something which isn't at all rare in international practice, e.g. the Euro. Whoever gave us one drachma we would give them back one euro. That is what happened in the beginning of the 1990's with the Argentinian peso. So as to be confronted, they said, inflation would be added to the dollar. One peso=one dollar and the opposite. This occurred with the bright sparks down at the IMF!

The Results are Well Known.

The problem of the Argentinian economy was found in its currency? A big deceit. A case of fetishism, which we come across only in the field of religion. Where the painter of holy images paints Mary and falls down on his feet in front of his piece of art and asks for himself to be saved! Thus man in society and commercial production has lot from his eyes his true relationships with his co-citizens and the division of labour among them, due to common survival and fantasizes that his life is determined not by the relationship with his co-workers but by other creations e.g. from a printed piece of paper, like the peso, which in and of itself has minimal value.

The diagnosis is wrong and the medicine chosen also. The patient wasn't the typed piece of paper as is always to be believed by monetarist bourgeois economics but in the given situation the low level of competition of the Argentinian economy in the international arena. The medicine chosen for the peso to become as hard as the dollar, without having in the background the dynamism of the US economy, the only thing it could achieve was to destroy totally the competitiveness of the Argentinian economy. As exactly happened.

Argentina had to travel backwards; its peoples had to suffer for a decade, to go bankrupt essentially for 75% of the debt to be written off, to disconnect the peso from the dollar and for it to be devalued, for the economy to start to develop once more. Naturally the problem wasn't solved permanently as the Argentinian economy is part of the world economy and in conditions of world crisis they cannot but influence all the national economies. The abandonment of the policy of the hard currency in Argentina ended up being the correct and imposed choice.

With Greece before WW2 the same had occurred. Venizelos as well in the name of anti-inflationary targets latched the drachma onto the British pound and later onto the dollar. As a result imports made money instead of exports; the deficits grew alongside the debts. Venizelos (no relation to current Economics Minister!) responded with an intensification of direct taxation, with sackings, cuts, autarchy and violence. In 1932 the country was forced to declare bankruptcy, taking the drachma off the link with the dollar and devaluation. Due to the policy that he followed the Liberal party imploded and Venizelos was forced to junk in his political career. From his ridiculous insistence on the hard drachma the political duet of Glyxbourg (ex-King) – Metaxas whilst the dictatorship that followed led the borrowers that Greece would continue to pay its debts.

Like Argentina in our days, Greece not only did not destroy itself, as the pre-war Cassandra's predicted but with a weapon the national monetary policy and its refusal to continue to pay this odious debt, it added phenomenal rhythms of development taking on the third highest on the planet after Japan and the Soviet Union!

What is the difference of coming out of a link with whatever hard currency (or from the hard Euro – if that was the relationship) from the forced or chosen exit from the Eurozone? None whatsoever. Let them not say that there isn't a historical parallel that we don't have experience and we don't know what the consequences are going to be for a return to our national currency.

I have referred to two examples but there are tens of others. Let those who sell catastrophism sell it to those who have no clue. We will not allow Greece and the Greek nation to disappear so some can sell slavery to the Euro-Atlantic bosses defending either which way the condemned Eurozone.

Unfounded Catastrophist Syllogisms

In the press and the internet one finds syllogisms against the return of the drachma, but one doesn't find many arguments. That isn't a coincidence. I haven't searched extensively but to the extent that I did, I found four paragraphs by Petros Dukas with which he tries to convince us that a return to the Drachma will be catastrophic. For all those that don't realise relatively that he was Deputy Minister in two New Democracy govt's, he studied economics and international relations in George Washington University, company management and finance economics at Columbia University and economics in New York University, to which he became a doctor of Economics. He also worked for Citibank in New York and became the general manager for the same bank in Greece.

P. Dukas supports that:
"The discussion and the threatening dilemma for a return to the drachma are unintelligible and self-destructive for our country. Further down he posts the first attack we will be forced to accept as Greeks!
The points numbered are Dukas the answers are mine.

1) We will constitute acceptance that us Greeks have totally failed, that we are unable to compete and we are in the 3rd Division of Europe

As Greeks were never asked or questioned if they wanted Greece to become a member of the EEC. Any who had a basic understanding knew that Greece was being thrown into a wolves den, as without trade protectionism it was impossible to compete with the west-European mega giants, when essentially, without the nations being asked, the rule of common market preference on the basis which the Union occurred, never functioned as this is how the uncontrolled centres of power in Brussels decided. Even worse there never were any European trade boundaries. With the GATT agreements and later the WTO ones the European market was transformed officially into a united world market, without the nations being asked. The entrance of Greece in 2001 into the Eurozone was the last nail in the coffin of the Greek economy. The fate of the Greek economy had been judged and that was known by all our politicians (amongst which is Dukas) unless of course we are to accept they are chosen simply by the level of dumbness.

2) The 'New Drachma' would unavoidably become immensely devalued in order to be able to aid the competitiveness of our exports. But never before has devaluation had anything more than medium term successes. It led to a cycle of inflation, a fear of a new devaluation, exit of capital and finally new devaluations.

Above the doctor of economics and deputy minister of economics (let us not forget that one) tells us that "we failed totally, that we are unable to become competitive and we are falling into the 3rd Division" But in paragraph 2 we accepted that the devalued drachma will "aid the competitiveness of exports" and consequently accepts that the overvalued for Greek measures euros will undermine our competitiveness. This doesn't stop him arguing (totally illogically) that the return of the drachma is destruction! He must assume that he is talking to idiots…

Fear Mongering Nonsense

Where does it come from that the devalued drachma equal's inflation? Or that more inflation brings about more inflation and that is why we will have capital flight abroad? All of this isn't but nonsense with which our esteemed Dr. is trying to frighten the people.

Inflation develops when we have few goods in the market in relation with demand hence we have an increase in prices. Or when the country is forced to print money from air as it has created obligations where its actual government coffers aren't able to service.

The new drachma will be devalued in relation not to itself but from its original price 1Euro=340.75Drachma s which it was on 1st January 2001. Not because it is written in its DNA but because it is to the interest of the country. It must because Greece became an open border paradise and lost all its rights handed over to foreign centres of power with the Euro hanging on its neck and lost as a result 50% of its competitiveness.

There will be repercussion which will occur on life, but they will only be positive. If the German Euro can't be devalued for the Greek terrain, the quislings that rule us found the answer in devaluing our lives. How else are we going to feed the usurers and we save the Eurozone which is one step away from death! They are taking the last cent which is circulating in the country having provoked a depression, mass unemployment, they cut and cut again salaries, pensions, they have unleashed a fierce tax chasing mechanism, the make incessant and constant increases in fuel, the prices of all utilities, the prices of all the basic basket of goods, they destroy the welfare state, all the services linked to people, health, education, everything.

The "New Drachma" which will replace the Euro will have the same form one euro = one new drachma which should become a paper note, with the same subdivisions and paper multipliers so as to avoid whatever speculation against the consumers. Whatever could be bought with one euro should be bought with one drachma. A wage of 800 Euros will become a wage of 800drachmas. The necessary devaluation is related to the relationship of the drachma with the euro and foreign currencies. In 2001 it was 1E=340drachma. Due to the economic meltdown which the country has suffered whose fault is due to the corrupt political personnel this relationship will change in defence of the drachma if we want to promote our exports and tourism. 1 Euro can become = 440.75drachmas. This devaluation in relation to foreign currencies is obviously going to influence to an extent the internal prices of the market, but not in a country where the govt will utilise all the possibilities internally and our relationships with abroad. We must add that a return to a drachma on its own does not satisfy for the country to stand on its feet. It must constitute the beginning of a new course, the independent and national domination of Greece, ready for new openings and open to fruitful co-operations with new peoples all over the planet, on the basis of mutual gain alone.

To proceed further: which exit of capital and fear of inflation is Dukas talking about? There are around $350 billion euros and dollars in the bank of Greece. There are the trading reserves of the country and not one has the right to touch them. If the state has the will it is in the position of defending them. Let us forget about capital flight. Neither Argentina in our days nor Greece in 1932 confronted such issues with bankruptcy and will not confront them now. The planet as a whole is facing the most complicated the most explosive crisis in its history and there are no areas which are now secure for any currency in any country. If capital flight occurs in Turkey which has its own currency the same will occur in Greece...

3) The massive debt in Euros should be paid in devalued drachmas. As a result our debt will increase to around 250% of GDP! Will the doctor of economics drive us mad: Given the fact that the 'massive debt' won't anyway be paid back (everyone understands that) not only is the debt transformed into drachmas but so does the GDP. Therefore the relationship of debt to GDP, remains constant, it doesn't change because we change currency.

4) All the citizens with investments and deposits in our country would aim to avoid the losses incurred from a return to a Drachma

and would take out quickly all the capital abroad with the result being the immediate collapse of the banking system and economic activity!

The respect and worth of a currency of a country is determined by the productivity of work but also by the quality of the productive goods. It improves or deteriorates from the development of these two factors. If they impose a currency on you like the Euro whose respectability and its price in the markets is very high as it is based on German competitiveness and quality, then it is truly illogical and an unnatural situation as it weakens severely exports, as he accepts in the 2nd paragraph and supports imports. With the Euro Greece has a permanent date with bankruptcy. We need a 180degree turn and one of the first measures for the country on the road to development is a return to a cheap drachma. When that occurs we won't have capital flight or investments from the country. The New Democracy 'doctor of economics' deceives aims to influence the Greek people. With the cheap drachma capital will flood into the country. If the opposite occurred as is being alleged we wouldn't see American and European capital emigrating to China with the cheap Renminbi but Chinese, Korean and Taiwanese to be emigrating to Western Europe and the USA!

As for the banks we say going bankrupt one after the other from the epidemic in the USA and Un Kingdom that occurred not because of capital flight abroad (so as to find safe ports, where truly?) but because we have a lack of liquidity, as their reserves are 'toxic' they are obligations by debtors who cannot pay. That is why every now and again states are making injections of liquidity in the banks so as to keep alive the money of its citizens. That occurs because it is in the nature of the market (which has been deliberately deified) cutting things down to size or increasing as it sees fit. The market is a creation of man and his creation; it cannot regulate the life of its creator. The creator man will tomorrow regulate the market and thus his life.
August 2011

(iii)The Greek Left on the European Community in 1961

In 1958 EDA (legal front of Left ie the banned KKE) became the official opposition with more than 24% of the official polls

Regarding the negotiations of Greece joining the European Economic Community from 1959 EDA emphasised
a)…with the entrance of Greece into the Common Market we had a very big leap towards the total political and economic subjugation of the country towards the foreign monopolies. The underdeveloped Greece is being thrown to the wolves of the powerful west european trusts and above all the west German ones..
The fate that will befall our agriculture won't be better. It will face violent competition of Italy, France and its colonies. An awful future awaits our future… If today the unemployed are more than 250,000 in the future that will double'

*

After the announcement of the an agreement being reached to join the EC, the ruling council of EDA on (31/3/1961) stated the following:
b) 1. The agreement of uniting Greece with the Six of the Common Market constitutes really a stage in the history of the country. Not towards the raising of the living standards of the Greek people as they rally regarding the event as shown by the PM but towards the opposite direction: the fierce intensification until immisserisation of the standard of living of the Greek people as the Greek economy via its integration becomes transformed into a typical area of colonial exploitation of the large monopolies of the countries of the EEC.

2. EDA from the first moment it became known that the govt wants to unite Greece with the countries of the Common Market expressed its full opposition towards this and from that day hasn't stopped fighting for its overthrow…

3. EDA considers the situation disastrous for the Greek economy and the Common Market as

a) The industrial and agricultural production of the country will be open to double deadly competition from the Six countries and will be erased...

b) Agricultural production despite what is being proclaimed to deceive the hardworking farmers will suffer industrial and other biotechnical consequences and instead of increasing Greek agricultural production we will end up in a contraction of Greek agricultural produce...

1960's protests for Democracy which led to 1967 American backed Junta

(iv) The Left Knew=Parliamentary Committee on Mass Immigration 1993

The Left knew there would be a massive problem in Greece they are co-signatories to this Parliamentary Committee (1993) both Syrizas predecessors Sinaspismos and the KKE. They didn't integrate or unionise the first thousands of illegals that arrived. They allowed through their leadership in unions for the situation to spiral out of control. We have now had riots in two major cities untold citizens committees being created on the issue and they are concerned alongside the Troika only about Golden Dawn, the retro fascist fake nationalists in order to give themselves a boost. When an indigenous working class is overrun by a similar number of illegals then a national question re-emerges. How one deals with this and what will happen next we leave to history. Suffice to say when Greeks are being killed on average 5 a month by illegals it wont be peaceful...

VN Gelis

GREEK PARLIAMENT
Crossparty Parliamentary Committee
For the study of the demographic problem of the country and the presentation of proposals for their more serious confrontation.

CONCLUSION

Chairman Vasileos Sotiropoulos Argolida MP New Democracy
Vice President Vasileos Geratidisi Thessaloniki B' COnstitutency PASOK
Secretary Manolis Drettakis A' Dsitrict Athens MP, Sinaspismos

Athens
February 1993
The demographic Problem of Greece and the proposals for confrontating It

Page 1
In our country which has one of the lowest birth rates the demographic problmes takes important national characteristics which may *threaten our national independence and territorial integrity*

Page 2
In the National Committee we also discusees two further questions of Manolis Drettakis (12/279 and 14/2/86) plus proposal of laws of MP's of PASOK 'motivations for the confrontation of the demographic problem of the country' on 7th and 28th November 1991.
Committee Members
1. Σωηρόπουλος Βασίλειος
2. Ανδρακτάς Παναγιώτης
3. Βαρδαρινός Βασίλειος
4. Γεωργολιός Κωνσταντίνος
5. Κανελλοπούλου Κρινιώ
6. Καραγκούνης Ανδρέας
7. Μπακογιάννη Ντόρα
8. Πάλλη Πετραλιά Φάνη
9. Παπαγεωργόπουλος Ελευθέριος
10. Παπανικολάου Ελευθέριος
11. Τατούλης Πέτρος
12. Χωματάς Ιωάννης
13. Γερανίδης Βασίλειος
14. Κρητικός Παναγιώτης
15. Κωνσταντινίδης Ελευθέριος
16. Μπαλτάς Αλέξανδρος
17. Παπαδόπουλους Βασίλειος
18. Παπαθεμελής Στυλιανός
19. Πάχτας Χρήστος
20. Σμπώκος Ιωάννης
21. Δρεττάκης Μανόλης (EAP) Sinaspismos (Syriza predecessor)
22. Κοσιώνης Παναγιώτης (KKE)

The members of the Committee Andreas Bakoyianni Dora, Palli Petralia Fani were replaced later, due to them undertaking ministerial duties from the MP's Theodoro Georgiadis, Dimopoulos Demetrios and Theodoro Katsiki whilst the position of the recently deceased in July 1992 Papadopoulos Vasiliou was received by the MP Skoulakis Emmanuel.

Pg 15
The repatriation of political refugees and the mass arrival of compatriots (Pontion and Northern Ipirus) with a correct political intervention will have positive results. The state should help them base themselves and work, not only in the city centres but also in the agricultural and semi-agricultural areas and to provide a new dynamic to many agricultural areas primarily in Northern Greece. The common cultural roots and Orthodoxy whouls help them adapt and assimilate into Greek society.

Particular attention should be place by the entrance and employment of tens of thousands of foreign immigrants legal (but mostly illegal) arrive in our country in the two last decades. Whilst the percentage of unemployment is around 8% in many sectors there is a lack of labour hands which has been covered primarily by foreign illegal immigrants.

With the illegal arrival of immigrants – mostly muslims from Afro-asian countries, Greece is being transformed into an area of receiving immigrants which creates social economic problems (conflicts in the labour market, increase in tax evasion with many consequences in the national insurance coffers, an increase in criminality, movement of drugs etc.) and they can't adapt to Greek society due to their totally different culture of Islam, which isn't simply a religion but a way of life.

Page 24
-The distance from the traditional forms of life and the arrival of events of social decay with the undermining of the principles of marriage, family life and children have a significant influence on the demographic issues.

-The highest form of individualism, the weakening of morality, drugs, AIDS and generally the social undermining and the world insecurity influence negatively the demographic problem.
-Future population development of Greece

Page 27
If the demographic indicators aren't improved and the same indicators of birth in 1990 (1.4 roughly average children per woman) and if they don't develop significant events (war, immigration) then the total population of the country in 2015 will be reduced by 500,000 people from todays numbers. The increase in these demographic indicators which started in 1985 creates severe problems of population in our country. The empty spaces which are created cover by a larger part from Pontius and Nothern Ipirus but also from muslims from Asia and Africa and from others who illegally enter Greece (and remain with a variety of fake conditions adding new problems)

Social-economic factors which influence the demographic problem.

Demographic consequences

Page 30
Our country with the dramatic reduction of births in the last decade has the possibility of big dangers (which are being intensified due to the geographical position and the lack of cooperative peoples);
-The reduction of births in the 1980's decade whereby the indicators fell from 2.09 children per woman to 1.4 in 1990, threatens quite severely the re-birth and continuation of our Greek race.

-The demographic gaps which are created in various geographic areas (Aegean islands, Ionian etc) have as the danger to be occupied by immigrants (mostly Muslims) with sever endless consequences.
-In the armed forces we will create serious problems with the lack of numbers of those in the armed forces.

Page 31
If for the re-birth of our labour dynamic and generally the course of

our economy and our social security we are based on the immigrants from Asia and Africa very soon we will have serious problems of social and national

Aims of Greek Demographic Politics - Proposals

Pg 36
-To emphasise at every available moment Greek tradition and religious feeling (practically with proposals of the Church)

Administrative measures

Page 40
-The illegal and easy entrance of illegal immigrants from countries of Asia and Africa either directly or via other countries of the EU must be observed closely for many socialeconomic and national reasons. There must be severe control regarding the legality of the entrance in our country and the legal presence and employment.

Athens 10th February 1993

The Trotskyist left which has a long and hard struggle in Greece never ever contemplated that the economic level of Greece could produce Nazism or the equivalent in history of German imperialism. Not because there was some ideal belief in the nature of the working population but because imperialism as an economic system was settled by the end of WW1. No new imperialism would emerge which could override or surpass the old imperialisms of the 19th century, bar the USA. In countries of a low socio economic development the bourgeoisie unable to rule directly usually rules via the army which many times takes on a bonapartist role (ie it acts above classes on behalf of the ruling class as a collective expression of the bourgeoisies will in periods of acute economic and social crisis). The current emphasis on the militarists of Golden Dawn is made to alibi the current quisling regime of the Troika to give it anti-fascist credentials at the same time as it is implementing outright fascist measures ie economic genocide. GD would have been unheard of if the political clowns that make up Antarsya and elements of Syriza weren't their marketing agents turning an insignificant grouplet which numbered no more than 2-300 organised people into a national political force by 'campaigning' against them constantly as if they are …fighting fascism and not in practice promoting it. So the theory goes that Greece would default create an army and march on Brussels and sort them out for turning the population into the beggars of the EU much in the same way as happened to Germany as a consequence of Versailles.

'We became Immigrants in our Areas'
Protests in central Athens districts

(v) From the Archives
Pouliopoulos on the Nature of Greek 'Fascism'
Translated by VN Gelis

The Dictatorship of the August Fourth Written in July 1939 in Akronafplia

1. The Metaxas dictatorship of 4th August has now completed 3 years of rule. In this period the bourgeois parliamentary parties were erased from the political scene. The organisations of the working class were dissolved and most of its militants were either in exile or imprisoned. The proletariat didn't express any resistance. Metaxas organised national labour unions and agricultural cooperatives on the basis of the 'leadership principle' and a hierarchy like Mussolini and Hitler. He every now and again organises popular demonstrations where he is declared to be the first worker, the first farmer etc. of the country. In the Administration, in Education, even in the Church, he implements the same bureaucratic totalitarian policy of autarchy in the economic field, just like fascism and he hasn't been slow to show his energetic support towards the fascist countries – including in trading with the Nazis. In the controlled press, in schools, in universities - everywhere - Metaxas has established the dominant ideology of the 'absolutist' state, of anti-communism, anti-liberalism and anti-capitalist demagoguery. Finally he created paramilitary units, just like those of National Socialism and Fascism. The whole political life of the country permanently revolves around what Metaxas says and does. Thus Greece became a Fascist country, with a Duce, a Fuhrer, Ioannis Metaxas. Such observations like the above were made by Stalinism. Such were also made by various Fourth Internationalists.

2. Stalinism didn't require as many signs as above to see Fascism appearing from the royalist proclamations of the 4th August 1936 when Parliament was dissolved. From the era of the "twin brothers" (Fascism and Social Democracy) and the

'Fascist' Bruning and before, they had characterised as Fascist, according to the period: Venizelos, Kondilis and Tsaldaris and every government which passed anti-labour legislation or overturned the so-called democratic freedoms of Bourgeois Democracy or Parliament. And the leading members of the KDEE (State-Capitalist, Stinas) needed a few months to pass after these events so they could raise a whole series of 'new political tasks'. This they incorporated into a new programme so as to justify the creation of the 'Workers Internationalist Party of Greece', as they declared in their official illegal bulletin. I summarise these tasks because that is imposed on us by the political reality (of imprisonment): due to the defeats of the workers by the fascist regime, they say, we must limit ourselves to communist propaganda, to cadres operating with all the restraints imposed by illegality and to wait in particular foreign victories of the European proletariat before we can re-propose active political slogans against the Dictatorship. As this was followed by the defeats in Spain and France, mass direct action against the Dictatorship became a political impossibility for an indeterminate future period. Stalinism produced different conclusions from the same characterisation of the government of the 4th August. The KKE sold out the rebellious workers in Thessaloniki on 9th May 1936 to the supporters of Metaxas and the Liberals. And it supported Sofoulis in the Parliament. This gave power to General Metaxas. They then called on the bourgeois parties to form an alliance with them against the Dictatorship. The raise the 'antifascist democrats' reactionary officers and overemphasises the chauvinism of Metaxas with indescribable socialpatriotic cynicism.

3. The practical result of this 'antifascist' policy has been the total erasure of the Fourth Internationalist KDEE within the first six months of the Dictatorship. It isn't the case that this total disappearance - from the beginning of 1937 - was due to numerical and organisational weakness. In fact, its leaders and some of its members were free and it even had the technical capability to publish illegal documents. These comrades had been instilled with a spirit of defeatism,

political indifference and reductionism: 'nothing can be done'. The practical result of Stalinist 'antifascism' was that most of its leaders and members were untouched by the regime: 90% of the CC and of the central and local cadres, their parliamentary leader, their second in command, MP's and prospective MP's and their regional committees, and theoretical leaders such as Glinos were free in Athens, in his case guaranteeing he wouldn't bother the government. The KKE officially declared for the 'patriotic policy' of the Dictatorship, "for the defence of the borders from external and internal enemies" and became followers of Metaxas' Okhrana. The Sklavenas-Sofulis agreement found its logical consequence in Sklavenas-Metaxas and this a long time before the KKE, first of all the democratic parties shook hands with the Palace and the British backed liberal George II.

4. If the proletariat were to choose either one of these two policies, the Workers United Front pessimism and the Stalinist Social Betrayal, it would be incapable of overthrowing the Dictatorship and to proceed to its historic liberation from the capitalist yoke. We believe that such a dilemma isn't currently in front of it. So the political considerations are to a great extent unclear and pessimistic and the Stalinist conclusions mistaken. If they told us only that a regime which abolishes parliament and dissolves workers organisations must be called fascist, as most liberal bourgeois have done in all the totalitarian countries, it would then be just a question of choosing the most suitable propagandistic label. But the question isn't the name, despite the social bases and political support of the current dictatorial government in Greece, as well as our tasks in confronting it. It is also known to us that confusion and the double edges in conditions which we always use, we end up with a mistaken confused opinion for the determined situations.

5. We all agree that there are differences within the dictatorship of 4th August and in the regimes that dominate today in Germany and Italy. But the truth is that what basically characterises both these regimes doesn't exist in Greece.

Even were we able to talk about the 'Fascism of 4th August', our political conclusions would be very different. In those countries the dictatorship is an agency of finance capital and the 'still hungry' imperialists, which is based on a big social base: pettybourgeois (post war dust) and workers masses disappointed by their experience of democracy (workers who are in provisional despair from the revolution which was sold out by the Social Democrats and the Stalinists). From here came the mass and paramilitary organisations (the basis on which these dictatorships to a large extent rely on) and from there we had vicious bureaucrats who comprise fascist and national-socialist unions and 'professional associations': and an alleged new state. This mass base fascism can to a greater or lesser extent be occupied either before or after its coup. It presupposes a long experience of the petty bourgeois masses from bourgeois democracy and bourgeois parliamentarism and a partial despair from the conditions of post-war bankruptcy of this parliamentarism. It is also sure that the enraged petty bourgeois masses are used against the proletariat. Fascism deceives them and contains them by means of a very effective organised social and chauvinist demagoguery. In these countries, due to their economic and technical coordination, the objective possibilities allow them, for a period of time, to carry out economic experiments known as 'totalitarian autarchy'. Despite the protestations of various circles, rotten capitalism in these countries provides sufficient to allow expansionist war preparations. They accept and support even this policy of economic isolation as a situation of extreme emergency. On the basis of such economic, social and historical conditions lies the relative stability of the regime. They explain the relative domination of the bourgeois and pettybourgeois intelligentsia (in Germany and many Junkers (the big landowners in Germany translators note) inside the political, administrative, military and educational hierarachies of fascism. Thus fascism in those countries became the only party of the national bourgeoisie, but it permanently despairs about the excessive cost which the overbloated parasitic administration of fascism spends. Despite this it is known that the accumulations of internal contradictions which is expressed and highlighted by the fascist pyramid, is being undermined, more and more threatening contradictions are being accumulated from their own policies which will blow the pyramid apart with either revolution or war.

Outside of the above essential features this particular from of class absolutism of monopoly capitalism called fascism can't be understood. This particular character of fascism in its birth and its historical development has been analysed scientifically by the Communist International's 3rd and 4th Congresses and by Trotsky from 1931-38 – including comparing fascism and the current Soviet regime in his work Revolution Betrayed. Never did the Left Opposition and the 4th International tire of emphasising that we don't have fascism when every dictatorship dissolves the labour organisation and attacks democratic freedoms. If we do, we confuse every form of absolutis, we don't aid in a more clear understanding of the many varied and contradictory political developments which fill our era or the more precise determination of the corresponding tasks of the revolutionary proletariat.

Which of the above characteristics exist in Greece and Romania eg in which other country of the Balkans where we have to a smaller or lesser extent destroyed or abolished parliaments, where the Courts rule with military-political cliques? None. That is why the sister party of our French organisation, last year, when writing about the Rumanian dictatorship of Karl, had called it not fascist, but Bonapartist. And of course the attacks against the workers' movement elsewhere is done by fascism, but here it is done by dictatorships of Kings and their cliques, even if we can call many of their measures 'fascist'. Despite all of their fascist trappings, the Bonapartist regimes aren't governed by the same historical laws nor do they follow the same path.

Here the masses never had the time, as in Western bourgeois democracies, to be so disillusioned by Parliaments so as to pass over into 'counterrevolutionary despair'. They maintain their relative illusions untouched to a large extent. With all the disillusion in their old parties and with all their distrust to the old leaders, the literature of Metaxas leaves the masses untouched and they are still waiting for their parties, despite the fact that now they have fallen prey to political apathy. The fact that Metaxas lasted three years and wasn't able to manage an administration of his own nor even a ruling party coalition – his political friends left his and the composition of the government appears to be a ship in stormy seas which every now and again throws the passengers into the sea – this shows how wrong is the estimation of the power of the dictatorship, characterising it as fascism.

Pandelis Pouliopoulos

(vi) December 2012

Submitted to CAFÉ (Campaign Against Federalism in Europe)

GREECE: A Nation State in its Death Throes
Exclusive report by VN Gelis

Having fought an election on the platform that 'there is money' PASOK's US-born leader, ex-Premier George Papandreou, fiddled the books and ensured the Greek budget deficit became larger than it was for Eurostat so that Greece could enter the IMF's bailout programme.*

Three years down the track, the aim of this subterfuge becomes increasingly clear: to create a new, tax-free, 'offshore', non-unionised region of the EU in the geographical territory that was Greece.

After 30 or so years of EU membership and a decade of Euro membership, for the last five years of which Greece has been in recession, GDP has collapsed by 25%, unemployment is officially around 25% (56% for youth, 33% in the private sector), soup kitchens and suicides (3,000 so far) are the only growth areas of the economy and the centre of Athens is starting to resemble parts of Detroit.

The last package of cuts—which cut wages by 50% for those still lucky to be employed and pensions by at least 25%—have the aim of dragging wages down to euro 300 and pensions to euro 100. The 'minimum' wage has been reduced. In the private sector, where workers are begging for work for as little as euro 10 a day for 12 hour shifts, 6 days a week, the minimum wage now stands at euro 580. Unemployment pay, which only lasts for a maximum of 12 months, stands at euro 360 with no housing component. This means that Greece is fast on the road to matching parts of Asia in wages so as to become the EU's role model for the future of the new regions the EU wants to create, which are to be run from the centre with new EU gauleiters in every ministry and every public institution (hospitals, universities and council offices administration), who will dictate budgets and cuts and have overall control, thus superseding both the Greek constitution and all local decision making.

As if to rub salt in the wounds, Greece has had the arrival of Germans, which is of course deliberate and conscious, to ensure the wounds of old (occupation of the Third Reich which led to 6-700,000 Greek deaths) are repeated in a new form.

The purpose is the total fire sale of all public assets, bigger in form than anything that has hit the Western world—including in countries which are or were the poster boys for neo-liberalism, Chile and the ex-USSR—with the eventual aim being the takeover of all public services in a deregulated, post-unionised, contract-based, private company paradise where workers will be employed only if willing to work for less and less. The process by which the Greek nation state is to be torn apart involves a changed electoral system under the Kallikratis Plan now being implemented. The plan created 13 regions of Greece with their own separate tax and spending powers and merged councils and town halls subordinate to the 13 regional governors who will decide policy directly for each region.

Germany recently proposed allowing German companies to employ Turkish citizens in Western Thrace (Greece) by allowing the relatives of those expelled in 1923 under the Treaty of Sevres to settle there, thus creating a new Kosovo in Greece. Proposals have also been placed on the table by the Troika to abolish Greece's standing army.

Depending on the resources each region has, privatisation lists are being drawn up. Assets are to be sold to transnational corporations for peanuts. For example, Skouries, in Thessaloniki, sold the rights to a Canadian gold mining company for a few million euros, it was then listed for hundreds of millions in a foreign stock exchange.

Despite over 20 general strikes—a genuine mass movement of occupation of city squares in the summer of 2011 involving millions of Greeks in over 30 cities—the ruling elite proceeds apace to impose EU directives as though they are confetti and to drive down lower than even the minimal alleged 'EU social charter'.

This is permitted because there is no minimum barrier for standard of living, health care or education. The enforced integration of Europe aims at creating one European government. This can only be accomplished by the abolition of the nation states, the centralisation of the banking system (three or four, controlled from the centre, will remain in Greece).

Thus, the formulation and implementation of policies of indigenous national development cannot occur. The implementation of the Bolkenstein directives ensured illegal immigrants worked on the building projects for the Olympic Games and that Greeks never got a look-in. Over euro 10 billion are exported to other countries via Western Union outlets as there are no capital controls.

Now that 95% of all building work has collapsed we have just the public sector left, which is the target of the large transnational corporations.

We have arrived at the stage where it has become clear that, instead of Greece's entry into the EU heralding development mirroring that of Germany, it has become de-industrialised and has lost nearly all its agricultural production due to EU directives and open borders in the importation of agricultural goods with zero tax, setting it on a path leading in the direction of Bangladesh. The perpetual race to the bottom has only one outcome. The effect will be to create the EU's first direct colonial region as the shining path for all others to follow suit—Portugal , Ireland , Spain.....

* Goldman Sachs helped the Greek government to mask the true extent of its deficit with the help of a derivatives deal that legally circumvented the EU Maastricht deficit rules. At some point the so-called cross currency swaps will mature, and swell the country's already bloated deficit.

In EU Connections with Goldman Sachs

Mario Monti Prime Minister of Italy who heads a technocrat government which replaced Berlusconi and is an international adviser to Goldman Sachs.

Mario Draghi Current Governor of European Central Bank and former managing director of Goldman Sachs International.

Lucas Papademos A former Prime Minister of Greece and had run the Central Bank during the controversial derivatives deals with Goldman Sachs when Greece hid the size of its debt.

Petros Chrisodoulou Began his career at Goldman Sachs and was head of Greece's debt management agency.

Otmar Issing Was a board member of the Bundesbank and Executive Board of the European Central Bank and an international adviser to Goldman Sachs.

Antonio Borges Is a former head of the IMF's European Department and former vice chairman of Golden Sachs international.

Peter Sutherland Was a former Attorney General of Ireland is a non-executive director of Golden Sachs International.

Karel van Miert Is a former EU Commissioner for Competition and former International adviser to Goldman Sachs.

Mark Carney Is the next Governor of the Bank of England. He was employed at Goldman Sachs for 13 years and became managing director of investment banking. He worked on South Africa's post apartheid venture into international bond markets and was involved with Goldman's with the 1998 Russian financial crisis.

Further examples welcome

other words Greece's debt was deliberately covered up with help from Goldman Sachs over a ten year period from 1998 to 2008.

OCCUPIEDGREECE
dispatches from behind enemy lines

(vii)No2EU Trade Information Group

April 2013

Cyprus: An EU Financial Coup?

VN Gelis

"The credit system, which has as its focus in the so-called national banks and the big money-lenders and usurers surrounding them, constitutes enormous centralisation, and gives to this class of parasites the fabulous power, not only to periodically despoil industrial capitalists, but also to interfere in actual production in a most dangerous manner…" "The Acts of 1844 and 1845 are proof of the growing power of these bandits."

Marx- Capital Volume Three (Chapter XXXIII):

From the bank bailouts in Greece (which have led to mass unemployment and immiserisation not seen since the last German Nazi occupation) we moved on to the bank bail-ins in Cyprus. It is a small island, a still divided ex-British colony with around one million Greek Cypriots and having a massive British military base on it. It became an offshore tax haven for the Russian neo-capitalist oligarchy (due to the dominance of AKEL – the Cypriot Communist Party). It entered the eye of the storm of the continuing Euro crisis in 2013. The ensuing events created essentially a break up of the Euro, transforming it into a two-tier Eurozone, with capital controls re-introduced in Cyprus, initially "temporary", but all the Troika measures of the last few years it ended up being permanent. Who is doing what to whom and for what ends are some of the issues to be analysed and what effect will they have on the Cypriot working class?

The bank heist was first announced for all deposits. But after the No vote of the Cypriot Parliament only for deposits in excess of E100k. More recently limits were placed on withdrawals less than this figure. It would thus take one person a full year to withdraw the 'guaranteed' deposit as withdrawals are limited to E300 daily. The official explanation was that Cyprus had 8 times too many foreign deposit holders, given the GDP of the country. The fact that Luxembourg has around 20 times for the same ratio raises the question as to why Cyprus was selected by the Eurogroup. Was it to warn Greece that if it goes against the EG that's what happens to you? Two banks, Laiki and Bank of Cyprus were targeted to be shut down by the ECB by winding down liquidity. Surplus banks, with surplus debts are to go the way of surplus products in capitalism, straight to the scrapheap, a policy akin to a scorched earth approach, with no respect to who it destroys in its path.

In the Greek crisis, workers were chosen as the excuse to bring in massive anti-working class attacks by the corporate mass media; in Cyprus the excuse was the participation of the Russian Oligarchs. Whilst the Troika arrived in Cyprus under the previous government of AKEL it was under the new government of Anastasiades and his ex-Finance Minister Sarris that this bail-in was agreed. The idea was to hold everyone responsible for the banking collapse (i.e. anyone and everyone with a bank account). We had the obscene spectacle of the banking system being closed for two weeks, the longest time for any country anywhere since WW2, whilst the people at the top shifted money out to Cypriot outlets based in the UK.

No Vote

Cypriot politicians voted NO to the attacks on bank accounts in Cyprus in order then to propose to 'save' bank accounts i.e. the minimum EU guarantee, but to block access to them. This was just a political charade and it was continued when Finance Minister Sarris went to Moscow to 'negotiate' when in reality he did nothing of the sort. It has been reported since that his relatives shifted money abroad! These politicians have agreed to bankrupt Cyprus and hand over all gas exploration rights to foreign multinationals. The issue becomes who will get them as the Russians no longer have a look in, so the struggle is between American and German firms. The rapprochement of Israel and Turkey was overplayed alongside Obama's visit as a counterweight to any ideas of not 'belonging to the West'. So small Cyprus has re-entered a dark neo-colonial financial meltdown and the coming attacks will be immense:

GDP is estimated to fall by 8% though it may be higher if there were more than 100,000 Cypriots employed in financial services of one sort or another and the recent cost of the bailout has increased from E17B to E23B i.e. another E6B magically added out of thin air:

E70 million in new property taxes

Business tax up from 10% to 12.5%

4.5% wage reductions for wages up to E1k

6.5% wage reductions for wages up to E1.5k

8.5% wage reductions for wages up to E2k

Reducing the public sector

Privatisations to bring in E1.4B from 2013-16

VAT from 17% to 19%

The current mythology perpetrated by the ruling economic terrorists is that all these economic measures will lead to some type of future growth. If Greece is anything to go by this growth has only been in suicides, mass unemployment and depression: nothing else. The other mythology is that these policies aren't a 'beggar thy neighbour' approach by the ECB to keep banks like Deutschebank standing last whilst everyone else is bled dry. Banks, like many consumer products under conditions of collapsing capitalism, are surplus to requirements. Cyprus was chosen on Greek Independence Day (25th March) as a warning to Greece: swallow whatever the Troika throws at you otherwise the 'Cyprus Option' will hit your banks as well. The EU is aiming to destroy the social fabric of society with the aim of buying up the island for a pittance after turning the population into scavengers. How the Cypriot population reacts will determine the real fate of these measures over the coming period.

The American clown Papandreou

December 2013
Greece: EU's Neoliberal Poster Boy
Economic Freefall

From a budget deficit at 120% of GDP in 2010 we are now hovering around 180% nearly four years into the worst crisis in living memory where GDP has fallen cumulatively by 25%, averaging 5% fall annually (whereas during the civil war it fell 12%!).

Unemployment has broken all EU records, hovering officially at 28% overall and 65% for the under 25year olds. Every year the claim is made that growth is returning, but the only growth on the horizon is unemployment (1.5m), soup kitchens, suicides (plus 5k) and homelessness.

Alleging they have created a budget surplus (by adding QE to the budget), the Government is being touted as the poster boy of the EU, but this has been done by reducing Greeks to penury. All new wages (including doctors) are at E580; the pension age has shot up to 67, with 40 year contributions. The latter essentially means the end of pensions for there is no work available for even a discontinuous 40 year period, though there is 'lots' of part time work. In other words, a decade after the arrival of the Euro, hourly wages are now at E2.5 (£2).

The EU's 'Free Movement' destroyed the Greek labour movement as Greece borders the ex-'communist' states of the Balkans. The oversupply of labour in a de-industrialising Greece led to a lowering of wages and the displacement of Greeks from the labour market. It is well known that Greece has large numbers of illegal immigrants who work in a cash economy and send euros abroad. Figures from the **Bank of Greece show that billions of Euros went to Albania, Pakistan and Afghanistan.** Of course figures on repatriation of funds by illegals is a kind of surrogate indicating the extent of the immigration as well as a scourge for the health of the Greek economy and Greek working people. In 2004 there were 4.5m active workers now there are 2m.

The cost of the Olympics and NATO's agreement that Greece should match Turkey's arms spending in the ratio of 7 to 10, essentially bankrupted the country. The added burden of 72 new property taxes and a collapse in property prices of between 30-80% has led to a 90% collapse in all new building work. This was the capitalist economic model of the last couple of decades and it appears to be in permanent decline.

Raw Materials: Gold, Gas & Oil: Bonanzas for Multinationals

The Greek gas distribution company Despa was sold to Americans not Russians, who offered a better deal, will not be functioning for years. A gold mine in Skouries, Thessaloniki, was sold for peanuts to a Canadian conglomerate by the ex-PASOK finance minister, Papakonstantinou, with no share (or even royalties) for the Government. Protestors have been imprisoned on trumped-up charges with demonstrations as large as 30k in Thessaloniki (Greece's 2nd city)

Health

The EU has done deals with Israeli pharmaceutical companies TEVA, via Germany, to import non-EU patented medicine for sale in Greece. The Greek pharmaceutical industry which employs over 20,000 people and supports over 30% of the domestic market will be shut down as a result. The model for this are the shipyards, airports and soon to be, railways and transport systems. The Samaras government is sacking contracted to the Greek NHS doctors by the hundreds (Finance Minister Georgiadis had a close escape in a meeting with them) and they have imposed E 25 charges to visit hospitals without taking into account the lack of medicines when one eventually manages to get into a hospital. The increase in mental health issues is such that, before the crisis, 1000 people yearly went to homes. Now it's more than 3000, but most of the mental health institutions are on the verge of closure due to lack of funding.

ERT-Public Sector

The State broadcaster, ERT was shut down in just 24 hours despite the lie that they would be re-hired. It has ceased international broadcasting as a prelude to total cessation of public sector broadcasting. Victory of the state here became the green light for further mass sackings (school caretakers, municipal police etc.).

The EU's rule means the imposition of externally determined budgetary constraints (25k sackings from the 700k strong public sector), making a public service media unviable. There is no other rule to require the existence of one so long as there is 'pluralism' i.e. more than one private sector provider of corporate 'news'. This is directly linked to the Free Trade Agreement with the USA which seeks the abolition of the 'cultural exception' of national governments in cultural life so that Hollywood dominates above all else. This is directed most strongly at France, but would apply to all European nations. The contemporary capacity to wage this cultural assault is in total contrast to the circumstances of 1939 when Greece won an important ruling against a Belgian company for a railway contract when it defaulted alleging if a public service is threatened states have the right to default. (1)

The EU is funding propaganda equating 'Nazism with Communism' under 'Europe for the Citizens' programme for 2014-20 whereby each nation's history is erased to create a 'common European citizen'. Participants (i.e. media outlets and NGO's) can claim up to Euro 100,000 for working towards this aim.

Massive strike wave
In the last twelve months strikes in the transport sector Metro, Seafarers and Secondary School Teachers, have been met with emergency strike bans in total conflict with all the agreements of the EU and ILO's alleged 'right to strike'. A strike by university administration staff facing sackings has been going on for 13 weeks with 3-4 of the main universities shut down for the last 3 months.

The conflict with the Troika and the collapsing Samaras government (which relies on 4 MPs to give it a majority) is now over continued mass sackings, repossessions of first homes and a land tax. As opposed to the rest of Europe, Greek home ownership was accrued primarily via work and not bank loans. So any new laws which aim to repossess properties on behalf of the parasitic banks will be met with fierce resistance, as has already been evidenced over electricity cut offs, imposed due to property taxes, which was eventually defeated on the streets. Thomson from the IMF said if you want a welfare policy buy tents.

The Troika, Agent of the ECB/IMF
None of the socio-economic indicators have improved over the four year programme and none of the declared aims have achieved anything more **than a massive worsening of standards of life.** The crisis has no end in sight despite all the official pronouncements and the contradictions building up in the foundations of the EZ are so large than when the debt crisis re-merges again(ECB's money printing ceases) it will make the previous one feel like a walk down the park. Only by breaking up the EU-EZ leaving its budgetary controls can nations embark on a different course. The irony is that the majority 'left' forces in Greece want a Europe of the 'peoples' whilst the euro-sceptics want a Europe of 'nations' when what is at stake that there is no common Europe for the common man but only for the multinationals and the centrifugal forces pulling it apart raises hope that the sooner it dissolves the better.

(1)"In a scholarly study on the issue of force majeure in relation to the obligations of States, Mr. Youpis (Greek council) explained yesterday that a State is not required to pay its debts if, by paying, it would compromise its essential public services. The Belgian government would most likely agree with the principle thus stated."

http://droit-public.ulb.ac.be/wp-content/uploads/2013/07/Working-Paper-The-ERT-case-or-when-a-screen-gone-blank-reveals-the-plight-of-public-service-in-Europe-a-documentary-breviary-to-fuel-the-debate.pdf

VN Gelis
6th December 2013

(viii) January 2014

The Real Reasons of the Catastrophic Crisis and the 'Left' Takis Fotopoulos

1. The integration of Greece into the EU is the real cause of its catastrophic crisis

The almost complete destruction of the lower classes in Greece is not due to the causes usually attributed to it by the "Left".[1] In fact, contrary to the misleading "explanations" provided by this Left and the Right alike, the actual cause is the full integration of the Greek economy into neoliberal globalization, through its accession into the EU. This has meant the complete transformation of Greece into an economic and political protectorate of the Transnational Elite.[2]

The catalyst for this crisis was Greece's unofficial default, which, however, was merely the consequence of the destruction of its production structure, as a result of the opening, and liberalization of markets imposed the EU, following Greece's entry in 1981. It is therefore no wonder that both the Left (apart from the Communist Left) and the Right—in fact, the entire Greek establishment—are fully united in not challenging the main cause of the present economic destruction: Greece's membership in the EU.

In other words, contrary to the deceptive pre-election promises of SYRIZA, (which is an organic part of the Euro-left that has just chosen its leader, A. Tsipras, as its candidate for president of the EU Commission), there is no way that an EU/EMU Member State could refuse to apply the policies imposed by neoliberal globalization, as borne out by History with Mitterrand, Lafontaine, Hollande, et. al. It is equally disorienting to state, as SYRIZA does, that, if elected to power, it would revert the catastrophic legislation imposed by the well known 'Troika' (representing the IMF, the EU and the ECB) in the past three years or so.

The above deceptive promises are based on the myth that neoliberalism is some kind of a mistaken ideology or a doctrine[3] upheld by "bad" politicians such as Thatcher, Merkel, Blair, etc. However, neoliberal globalization is, in fact, a systemic phenomenon implying, also, that the EU members' economic growth does not rely anymore mainly on the domestic market but on the international market (within the EU and without) and that it is the Trans-National Corporations (TNCs) that control world production and trade, and—through the Transnational Elite[4]—the international political, military and cultural institutions.

So, only if the EU governments were taken over by the Euro-Left and they then forced the TNCs based in EU to operate solely within the EU area—imposing in the process strict social controls on the movement of capital and commodities from the other economic blocks (i.e. those of the Far East and America)—only then could the European economy be indifferent to its own level of competitiveness and live in the Euro-Left's nirvana, happily ever after. In fact, however, EU is moving in exactly the opposite direction of further integration within the New World Order (NWO) defined by neoliberal globalization! This is clearly shown by the current negotiations between EU and US for a Transatlantic Free Trade Area.

2. Capitalist globalization can only be neoliberal

The Euro-elites simply cannot afford to lose more of their competitiveness. In fact, the real reason for the creation of EU and later of the Eurozone had nothing to do with the ideals of freedom, democracy, human values and the rest of its ideology, as EU's history has clearly shown. It was the growing gap in competitiveness (in terms of EU's share of world exports) during the 1980s, which led the Euro-elites to speed up the integration procedures, which were mostly dormant up to then. The EU economic failure was clearly due to the fact that the competitiveness of its commodities was increasing at much slower rates than those of is competitors, particularly in the low cost countries of the Far East.[5] As supporters of the EU and its integration were claiming at the time, only a market of continental dimensions could provide the security and the economies of scale that were necessary for the survival of the European capital in the hyper-competitive global market that was just emerging at the time.

However, despite the high degree of integration achieved by the 'Single European Act' in the 1990s, and even despite the creation of the Eurozone, its decline in competiveness continued. Thus, whereas the share of Euro-exports to world exports was 35.8% in 1990, ten years later, it has fallen to 29.7% and by 2010 it has fallen further to 26.3%![6] In other words, within two decades, the Eurozone countries have lost more than a quarter of their competitiveness, measured in terms of their share in world exports. Although the Euro-elites are well aware of the fact that a significant part of their 'loss' of exports is in fact due to their de-industrialization—because of the move of industrial capital by the TNCs (most of them based in the metropolitan countries including the Eurozone ones) towards the low-cost paradises of China, India and the rest— this is obviously no consolation to their own workers (and electorates), which benefit very little (if at all!) by globalization!

The present EU policies therefore, are not the result of a conspiracy or a satanic plot of the elites to exploit further the European workers but simply of the fact that the opening and liberalization of markets required by globalization, so that TNCs could expand their activities further, inevitably led to the present neoliberal policies implemented by every country fully integrated into the New World Order. To put it simply, globalization in a capitalist world can only be neoliberal and the rest is mythology adopted by today's bankrupt world "Left"––apart from the genuine (but diminishing) anti-systemic Left.

3. Competitiveness is the rule

If, therefore, we accept the premise that the Euro-elites have no other option but to improve their competitiveness within the globalized economy, the next question is how competitiveness can be improved. There are two main ways in which a country's competitiveness could improve: either by changing relative prices, i.e. squeezing the prices of locally produced commodities with respect to those produced abroad by squeezing wages and salaries, or by improving productivity of locally produced commodities, which may lead to lower cost of production without reducing real wages and salaries or to better quality products, etc.

Changing relative prices in the former way is the easy solution, as it could be implemented, almost at a stroke, in case a country controls its own currency and Greece itself has repeatedly resorted to devaluation policies in the post-war period to improve, temporarily, its competitiveness. In case however a country does not control its currency, as is the case of Greece in the Eurozone, the only other option, given its historically low level of labor productivity because of the lack of investment in research and development, is the presently implemented policy of squeezing wages and salaries in the hope that the cost of production will fall accordingly. In fact, the level of Greek productivity of labor, for instance has always been historically much lower than that of the Eurozone (in 2006 it was just 77% of the average Eurozone one[7]), something which is not that much peculiar if we take into account the fact that the proportion of productive investments to the GNP is much higher in the European 'North' than in the 'South' in general and Greece in particular.

So, if we start with the premise that the uneven levels of competitiveness and productivity are unavoidable in an economic union like the EU, which consists of countries at highly different levels of development (as they have been historically formed within a very uneven development process like the capitalist one), then we may easily understand the causes of the crisis in countries like Greece. The fact, therefore, that a Eurozone country like Greece, facing a problem of low competitiveness, cannot devalue its currency (i.e. change its relative prices without the need for suppressing domestic wages and incomes) is not the cause of the crisis. This may be the cause of a similar competitiveness crisis of an advanced capitalist country like Germany but not of a country like Greece where low competitiveness is a development problem.

Particularly so, when the Greek entry to the EU and later to the Eurozone had itself significantly exacerbated the development problem by effectively dismantling the productive structure of the country, as its infant industry and agriculture were not capable to compete with the imported commodities, following the opening and liberalization of markets imposed by the Single Market. Under these conditions, even a Greek exit from the Euro and a devaluation of the drachma that will be re-introduced in its aftermath, could only have temporary effects on Greek competitiveness, unless mass investment in its productive structure takes place at the same time, which is far from guaranteed in an internationalized market economy.

4. The EU as a mechanism to transfer surplus from its "South" to its "North"

In other words, competitiveness at the core Euro countries, which are characterized by higher levels of labor productivity than in the South, mainly depends on keeping wages and prices under control, so that German commodities continue to be competitive (because of their higher quality and so on) compared to similar commodities produced in East Asia and beyond. On the other hand, compettiveness in the European periphery, which consist of countries with lower levels of labor productivity, like Greece, mainly depends on improving productivity through new investment on R&D. Therefore, the competitiveness problem in the South is mainly a development problem and refers to the need of creating a strong productive base, which will not be formed within the process of uneven capitalist development (as today), but within a process of social control of the economy to create a self-reliant economy.

Yet, despite the fundamental difference concerning the causes of low competitiveness between the "North" and the "South" of the EU, in the framework of the post-Maastricht Europe, a common policy was adopted for all member countries—a policy that was determined by the needs and the interests of the North. Thus, the Single Market, did not mean the unification of peoples, as the EU propaganda presented it, not even the unification of states, but simply the unification of free markets. 'Free markets', however mean not only open markets (i.e. the unhibited movement of commodities, capital and laboutr), but also flexible markets (i.e. the elimination of any obstacle in the free formation of prices and wages, as well the restriction of state role in the control of economic activity, which implies the drastic restriction of the element of 'national economy'.

This was the essence of the neoliberal globalization characterizing the new institutional framework of the EU, i.e. that the state control of the domestic market of each member state (which was drastically restricted within the Single Market of 1992) was not replaced by a corresponding EU control of it, apart from some (mostly nuissance) regulations on uniformity, etc. In other words, the new institutions aimed at the maximization of the freedom of organized capital,, whose concentration was facilitated in any way possible, and the minimization of the freedom of organized labor, whose co-ordination was restricted in any way possible and mainly through the unemployment threat.

If Germany is indeed the country which was on the receiving end of the greatest benefits from joining EU and the Eurozone, whereas the countries of the European South received the least benefits out of it, this was far from accidental or due to the bad designing of the Eurozone as, post-Keynesians and other reformists (including the Euro-Left!) argue. When the Eurozone was institutionalized at the beginning of the new millennium Germany already enjoyed relatively high levels of labor productivity and competitiveness and the new currency essentially has 'frozen' the relative deviations between the advanced North of the Eurozone and the much less advanced South (parts of which were in fact underdeveloped).

Then, the Single Market itself, under conditions of a common currency, brought about a relative equalization of commodity prices and a certain increase in wages in the South, as workers were struggling to maintain the real value of wages and at the same time to narrow the gap in wages with Northern workers. On the other hand, German employers were in a much better position to suppress wage rises because of the difference in labor productivity they enjoyed due to advanced technology and investment in R&D, but also due to better relative prices. As Wolfgang Münchauput it, "Germany entered the Eurozone at an uncompetitive exchange rate and embarked on a long period of wage moderation.

Macroeconomists would say Germany benefited from a real devaluation against other members".[8] If we add to this, that the countries in the South no longer had the power to devalue their currencies, whereas Germany did not have any need to devalue its currency as long as it could keep wage rises in pace with labor productivity increases, then we can understand why (and how) the Eurozone essentially functions as an economic mechanism to transfer economic surplus from the countries of the European South to those in the North and particularly Germany.

5. The disorienting role of the "Left"

The obvious conclusion is that it is impossible to take any radical measures to exit from the current economic (and not only!) disaster, without a unilateral exit from the EU along with a cancelation of the debt (for which the people were never asked anyway), as well as the discarding of all legislation imposed by the Troika and the adoption at the same time of the necessary geostrategic changes. Only this way, Greece could retrieve the minimum required economic and national sovereignty for a strategy for economic self-reliance, which is necessary for the permanent exit from the crisis, through building a new productive structure to meet its needs.

This means that the views that we could implement another policy even within the Eurozone, as SYRIZA suggests, or that it would suffice to exit from the Euro (without the parallel direct and unilateral exit from the EU) to implement a radically different economic strategy (as other Left organizations suggest), are completely misleading. This is because, as I tried to show above, the cause of the present economic catastrophe in Greece is neither the austerity policies of the Troika, as the supporters of the former view claim, nor the poor design (and implementation) of the Euro that led us to deficits and massive debt, as argued by the supporters of the latter view.[9]

Thus, supporters of the former view (Laskos and Tsakalotos), in fact, reproduce the myths of an obsolete internationalism according to which the struggle of the European proletariat within the EU will reverse the austerity policies, despite the fact that, after almost five years of economic crushing of the popular strata, there has not been even a single ("official" or unofficial) European strike against these policies! On the other hand, the supporters of the latter view (Flassbeck and Lapavitsas), acting as the "Plan B" of the Euro-elite––in case it is forced to expel (temporarily or permanently) Greece from the Eurozone—argue for a Greek exit from the Euro, but not from the EU. However, in both cases, the failure of the proposed policies can be taken for granted, although the consequences will not be identical.

Thus, in the first scenario of a SYRIZA-based government (which looks likely following the Euro elections that could well function as a catalyst for general elections) it is a matter of time for its failure to become evident, if it insists on its pro-EU and pro-Euro policy. Despite its present rhetoric, it would simply have to follow the same economic policies as the present government, perhaps with a minor relaxation of austerity policies (assuming that the Euro-elites will find a way to cancel part of the Debt to make the rest of it payable). As markets will remain open and liberalized under a Syriza government (the party never challenged this fundamental tenet of neoliberal globalization), labor markets will also continue to be flexible. However, open and liberalized markets mean:

- wages and salaries will be kept at around their present minimum levels, or, at least, these levels will be the basis for any future increases strictly linked to productivity rises;
- Public Health and Education will never recover from their present dismantling, as the government will have to continue implementing the present Eurozone strict fiscal policies to keep budget deficits under strict controls;
- the selling out of the social wealth of Greece, following privatizations of essential services like electricity, water, transport, ports and airports, communications (and now even Greek islands!) will not be reversed, making the implementation of any effective social policy to protect the victims of globalization impossible;
- Unemployment may marginally fall from the present almost 30% of the working population (and 60% of young people) only to the extent that foreign investors will be attracted by

the present extremely low wages/salaries and the 'political stability' that SYRIZA might secure. However, given the strong competition on this front by other low-wage countries in the Balkans and beyond (East Asia), unemployment is bound to be stabilized at very high levels for any foreseeable future, with young Greeks having either to work in Greece's "heavy industry" (as the establishment calls tourism) or emigrate.

Clearly, this Latin-Americanization (or Balkanization) of the Greek economy will become permanent under SYRIZA's pro-EU policy, and in the elections to follow a (likely brief) period of SYRIZA in power, the party will probably have the fate of the social democratic party PASOK, which has effectively been demolished. In fact, this would simply be the belated end of the Euro-Left in Greece, following the similar end of this kind of "Left" in the rest of Europe, in the era of globalization. Yet, the International "Left" is unable to see all this and would be ready to celebrate the possible victory of SYRIZA in the next elections,[10] whereas Leo Panitch, is so enthusiastic about the new kind of 'progressive' reform SYRIZA represents that he became almost lyrical when reading that Tsipras "spoke in terms of the 'historic opportunity' that now exists for a left alternative to the current capitalist 'European model'.[11] This, at the very moment when the same Tsipras is also indirectly praised by the New York Times, the leading organ of the Transnational Elite, presumably as a 'serious' Left politician worthy of its trust, compared to the 'loony left' they so despise:

Mr. Tsipras…has backed away from past rhetoric about abandoning the euro and said he does not want Greece to drop out of the 18-country zone that uses the currency. But he does want a fundamental reworking of the terms of Greece's bailout funds, worth 240 billion euros, or about \$328 billion."Our intention is to change the framework, not smash the euro", he said.[12]

On the other hand, in the case of the second scenario, i.e. of a Left government that decides a Greek exit from the Euro (but stays in the EU), the image would be much more blurred, as the reintroduction and significant devaluation of the reintroduced drachma would initially bring in some positive results. But, these would be completely temporary, unless they were accompanied by a parallel radical restructuring of the productive structure, based on social decisions and not left to the market forces, as both scenarios implicitly or explicitly assume. And this brings us back to the need for a strategy of self-reliance that presupposes a Greek exit from both the Euro and the EU.

The main reason why both approaches are not only wrong, but also completely misleading, is that they are not based on the fact that the current devastating crisis is due to structural reasons having everything to do with the uneven capitalist development process, which is further exacerbated in the era of neoliberal globalization and the consequent policies implemented by the EU, and very little to do with the broader financial crisis[13], austerity policies, or the debt itself and the ways to deal with it .

Thus, as far as austerity policies are concerned, it is obvious that they are a consequence and not the cause of the devastating crisis. The solution, therefore, to the "problem" is not just the redistribution of income at the expense of profits and in favor of wages, as (supposedly is the conclusion drawn by a "Marxist" kind of analysis), as this inequality is nothing new but an inherent characteristic of the capitalist system. Unsurprisingly, despite growing world inequality during the era of neoliberal globalization, the system has enjoyed a sustained period of expansion throughout this period, with world GDP rising at an average 2.9% in the 1990s and 3.2% in the period up to the beginning of the latest financial crisis (2000-08)[14]. Furthermore, the only case that a systematic redistribution of income against the rich took place in a capitalist system was when the tax burden was shifted to the rich during the social democratic period (approx. 1945-1975). However, this kind of redistribution is simply not feasible anymore in the NWO of Neoliberal Globalization, since Trans-national Corporations can easily move to tax havens like Ireland, India, etc. leaving massive unemployment and poverty behind them.

Yet, neither the deficits and the consequent debts were created by reckless fiscal policies nor, as more sophisticated variations on the same theme maintain, because of the fact that the German elite were suppressing wage rises at a time when the other elites in the Eurozone, and particularly the elites in the Euro periphery, were doing the exact opposite. This policy, according to the same argument had created an artificial competitive advantage and consequent Balance of Payments (BP) surpluses in Germany and, vice versa in the European South, i.e. low competitiveness and BP deficits. This, in turn, had led to excessive borrowing by the peripheral countries, (made easy by the fact that it was backed up by a strong currency, the Euro) up to the moment that the fiscal "bubble" burst, when the consequent shortage of liquidity made lending to these countries much tighter, leading to the well known debt crises in countries like Greece. Not surprisingly, the Euro-elite, has just decided to adopt an even tighter economic control of the Euro-members, through the Banking Union.[15]

6. Concluding remarks

The crucial, therefore, issue arising is the following one: can a small Euro-peripheral country like Greece afford not to implement the policies of neoliberal globalization today? Or, should, (as the present "Left" suggests), the millions of unemployed and poor wait for a radical change in the balance of forces in the EU and the Eurozone, so that a new pan-European Left government proceeds with the 'progressive' reforms suggested by its supporters? Alternatively, should they better wait for a new socialist revolution in order to proceed with genuine socialist policies, as suggested by the dwindling anti-capitalist Left? My sympathies would of course be (as have always been) for an anti-systemic Left, as it is the only one which struggles against its full integration into the system and the NWO. Yet, it is obvious to me that, today, this Left is no less millenarian than the integrated into the system "Left", and as such is equally useless to the victims of globalization, who every day lose even more their hope for any better future, many of them increasingly resorting to suicide.

Under these conditions, it is clear to me that only if a country broke away from the internationalized market economy and pursued a policy of self-reliance, it could retrieve the necessary degree of economic and therefore national sovereignty, so that it is the people who will be determining the economic process, i.e. which economic and social needs are met and how, instead of leaving this life-and-death issue to 'market forces' and the Social Darwinism they inevitably imply. This, for a country like Greece would imply the need for the creation 'from below' of a Popular Front for Social and National Liberation[16] (instead of relying on the professional politicians of the "Left" or of the Right), which will formulate a program for the radical changes needed to achieve the short term aim of restoring full social control on all markets, unilaterally cancelling the Debt and all related legislation imposed by the Troika, as well as a unilateral exit from the EU. Although socialization of the banking system and of the de-nationalized industries, particularly those covering basic needs (energy, water, transport, communication, etc.) will be necessary even at this early stage, yet, the medium-term aim will have to be economic self-reliance, so that the basic needs of all citizens are met through the rebuilding of the economic structure according to social needs rather than according to market demand. On the other hand, the issue of the systemic change, i.e. whether Greece would be in the future a state-socialist society, an Inclusive Democracy,[17] or a radical kind of social democracy, will be determined by the people themselves at a later stage once the present crucial problems concerning their survival have been sorted out..

In fact, Greece will not be alone in such a struggle against the NWO and neoliberal globalization. Not only the peoples in other countries in the European periphery and beyond would follow its example when they realize that there is a way out of the present catastrophe, HERE and NOW, but also the peoples who already fight against neoliberal globalization would also join the common struggle against the New World Order of neoliberal globalization. In fact, this struggle is already intensifying from Latin America (Venezuela, Bolivia, Cuba, et. al.) up to the Eurasian peoples of the ex-USSR, and the peoples in the Arab countries (I do not of course mean the pseudo-revolutions in Tunisia and Egypt or the engineered insurrections in Libya and Syria),[18] who shed their blood everyday in the struggle for their national and social liberation.

Takis Fotopoulos *is a political philosopher, editor of Society &; Nature/Democracy and Nature/The International Journal of Inclusive Democracy. He has also been a columnist for the Athens Daily Eleftherotypia since 1990. He is also the author of numerous books in Greek on development; the Gulf War; the neo-liberal consensus; the New World Order; the drug culture; the New Order in the Balkans; the new irrationalism; globalization and the Left; the war against "terrorism"; His latest book in Greek is Greece as a protectorate of the transnational elite: The need for an immediate exit from the EU and for a self-reliant economy (Athens: Gordios, November 2010). He is also the author of over 1,000 articles in British,* American and Greek theoretical journals, magazines and newspapers, several of which have been translated into over twenty languages. His latest book is :Subjugating the Middle East. Integration into the New World Order (Progressive Press, 2014)*

Notes

[1] See e.g. the recent book by two members of the SYRIZA leadership, (one of them a member of Parliament representing the party), Christos Laskos and Euclid Tsakalotos, Crucible of Resistance: Greece, the Eurozone and the World Economic Crisis, (Pluto Press, Sept. 2013).

[2] Takis Fotopoulos, "Greece: The implosion of the systemic crisis", The International Journal of INCLUSIVE DEMOCRACY, Vol. 6, No. 1 (Winter 2010); see, also, Greece as a protectorate of the transnational elite,(Athens: Gordios, November 2010),http://www.inclusivedemocracy.org/fotopoulos/greek/grbooks _gordios_EE_2010/grbooks_gordios_EE_2010.htm

[3] see e.g. Naomi Klein, The Shock Doctrine:The Rise of Disaster Capitalism, (London: Penguin, 2008).

[4] see for the meaning and significance of the Transnational Elite in administering the NWO, Takis Fotopoulos, Subjugating the Middle

East: Integration into the New World Order – Vol. 1: Pseudo-Democratization, (Progressive Press, 2014), Part I.

[5] Thus, whereas the EU share of world exports was stagnant between 1979 and 1989 , the US share increased by 3.5% and the Far Eastern share increased by a massive 48% ,(World Bank, World Development Report 1991, Table 14).

[6] World Bank, World Development Indicators 2002, (Table 4.5) & World Development Indicators 2012, (Table 4.4).

[7] World Bank, World Development Indicators 2008, Table 2.4.

[8]Wolfgang Münchau, "Germany's rebound is no cause for cheer", Financial Times, 29/8/2010.

[9]Heiner Flassbeck and Costas Lapavitsas, Left-Wing Strategies to Solve the Euro Crisis, (Rosa Luxemburg Foundation:: Berlin, May 2013, http://www.rosalux.de/fileadmin/rls_uploads/pdfs/Studien/kurzfassung_flassbeck_en.pdf

and full version in "The systemic crisis of the euro – true causes and effective therapies", http://www.rosalux.de/publication/39478.

[10] See e.g. Andreas Bieler, "Crucible of Resistance: Class Struggle Over Ways Out of the Crisis", Socialist Project • E-Bulletin No. 926 January 10, 2014; Reproduced also in Global Research.

[11]Leo Panitch, "Europe's left has seen how capitalism can bite back»" , The Guardian, 13/1/2014.

[12]Andrew Higgins, "Opposition Dissent Tempers Greek Attempts at Optimism",

The New York Times, 12/1/2014.

[13] Takis Fotopoulos, "The myths about the economic crisis, the reformist Left and economic democracy", The International Journal of INCLUSIVE DEMOCRACY, Vol. 4, No. 4, (October 2008), http://www.inclusivedemocracy.org/journal/vol4/vol4_no4_takis_ec onomic_crisis.htm

[14] World Bank, World Development Indicators 2010, Table 4.1.

[15] 'Big step' reached in rescue plan for eurozone banks, BBC News, 12/12/2013 ; See, also, Maria Snytkova, "European countries lose bank sovereignty", English Pravda, 2012/2013 http://english.pravda.ru/world/europe/20-12-2013/126445-bank_sovereignty-0/

[16]see Takis Fotopoulos, "Neoliberal Globalization and the need for popular fronts for national and social liberation", The International Journal of Inclusive Democracy, Vol. 9, No. 1/2 (2013), (under publication).

[17]Takis Fotopoulos, Towards An Inclusive Democracy, (London/NY: Cassell /Continuum, 1997/1998).

[18] Takis Fotopoulos, Subjugating the Middle East: Integration into the New World Order – Vol. 2, Engineered Insurrections,(Progressive Press, 2014).

PASOK's finale soon to be followed by New Democracy...

(ix) Greece and the EU

Head of Euro Group Greece's problems started 30 years ago...

Greek Trade Deficits
1980 till 2008 Greece's trade deficit with the rest of the world went up 9 times
In current prices from £5.2b in 1980 it reached E44b in 2008 and E34b in 2009
In 1980 Greece had a surplus in its farming budget at 3.3b Drachmas but from 1981 the year it first joined the EU it went to a deficit to E290m. The deficit has now gone to E3b Euros an increase of 934%

Foreign Loans by Years
Foreign loans taken out in 1990 were equivalent to E694m
In 2000 equivalent to E7.16b
In 2009 equivalent to E85b
So by 2009 the Greeks were 1,009% more in debt than in 2000 (decade of the Euro!!)

Public Debts
In 1980 it was E600m
Three decades later it was E298b
The debt went up 497times in joining the EU

EU 'AID' to GREECE
Four major packages
-1986-1993 for E471m
-1994-1999 E12.3b
2000-2006 E26.1b
2007-2013 E27b
If one aggregates them all they equal to about E65b
In a period of 33years from the joining the EU Greeks 'received' 'aid packages' equivalent to 196Euros a year or 0.54c a day!

Greece's Trade Deficits with the EU
Imports equivalent to E379b for the three decades of entrance

Exports equivalent to E125b
Conclusion we gave them E254b for imports received E65b in 'aid'.
In other words for every Euro we received we gave back 5
Christine Lagarde = Greece's Deficits are Germany's Surpluses Oct
2010

Taken from the Greek book (Ειναι ο Καπιταλισμος Ηλιθιε) **'Its
Capitalism Stupid'** Nick Bogiopoulos-KKE

Articles on the Net:

THE GREEK CAULDRON http://newleftreview.org/II/72/stathis-kouvelakis-the-greek-cauldron

Alexis Tsipras Guardian interview http://www.theguardian.com/commentisfree/2013/nov/27/austerity-left-unite-europe-alexis-tsipras

Heather Gibson http://newpost.gr/post/171752/i-suzygos-toy-e-tsakalotoy-Heather-D-Gibson-logografos-kai-sumvoylos-toy-provopoyloy

Greek pseudo-left leader Tsipras auditions for State Department, IMF http://www.wsws.org/en/articles/2013/01/26/tsip-j26.html

Hilary Wainright Red Pepper- Syriza shines a light

Drachma not an Option-Interview with Tsipras http://www.athensnews.gr/issue/13512/58165

Bibliography

'Crucible of Resistance' Christos Liasko Euclid Tsakalaotos

'The Demystification of the Euro' Theodoros Katsanevas

'It's Capitalism Stupid' N Bogiopoulos

FT –If Greece Goes

Websites

http://aristerovima.gr/

http://left.gr/   **SYRIZA**

http://www.iskra.gr/

http://patari.org/

http://vngelis.blogspot.co.uk/   **Patriotic Left**

http://imfoccupationgreece.blogspot.co.uk/

List Price: **$12.50**

224 pages

ISBN-13: 978-1466399464 (CreateSpace-Assigned)

ISBN-10: 1466399465

BISAC: Political Science / Economic Conditions

An analysis about the role of the IMF in Greece coupled with many eyewitness reports for the first time published in the English language in one location. What is happening, how it happened and what might be the eventual outcome of this rape of a country and its people. The first book of its kind that charts the rise and fall of the Greek Indignants. Worth a read for all those disgusted and appalled at the global banksters treatment of nations in the current light of the growth of the Occupy Wall Street movement in the heart of the USA.

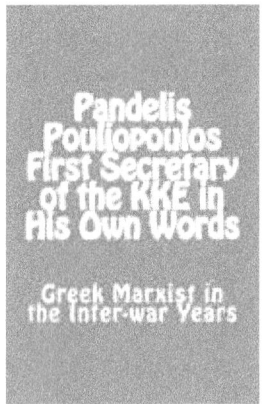

List Price: **$8.50**

248 pages

ISBN-13: **978-1470139940** (CreateSpace-Assigned)

ISBN-10: **1470139944**

BISAC: **Political Science / Government / General**

The premier marxist of Greece who led the War Veterans Association and was the first secretary of the KKE later joining Trotsky's Left Opposition

List Price: **$12.50**

242 pages

ISBN-13: 978-1468011548 (CreateSpace-Assigned)

ISBN-10: 1468011545

BISAC: History / Historiography

A collection of articles from a marxist standpoint, some written in the period of the Greek Civil War some written after, tryiing to analyse the roots of the issues and how one had to confront the first great attempt at the enforced unification of Europe under the iron heel of Nazi rule

List Price: **$15.00**

196 pages

ISBN-13: **978-1466360570** (CreateSpace-Assigned)

ISBN-10: **1466360577**

BISAC: History / Revolutionary

How the Russian Revolution influenced and gave rise to communist ideals in the Greek labour movement and the rise of the KKE-Greek Communist Party

ABOUT THE AUTHOR

The author has been involved with Greek political and economic history since he became politically conscious. He has published a series of books both with an emphasis on current political developments focusing almost exclusively on eye-witness reports and the role of the fake Left as well as information regarding Greece's history from the point of view of revolutionary political movements.

www.ingramcontent.com/pod-product-compliance
Lightning Source LLC
Chambersburg PA
CBHW060510290526
45791CB00001B/352